D1159834

**Learning About
NATURE
Through
GAMES**

prepared for
National Recreation and Park Association
by
VIRGINIA W. MUSSELMAN

STACKPOLE BOOKS

LEARNING ABOUT

NATURE

THROUGH

GAMES

Learning about Nature through Games

STACKPOLE BOOKS
Cameron & Kelker Streets
Harrisburg, Pa. 17105

Price: $3.95

Library of Congress Catalogue Card
No. 67-12927

Printed in U.S.A.

For my
Two little Great-Nieces
Laura and Stacy Musselman
and my
Two little Great-Friends
Andrea and Cynthia Bair

*   *   *

May they never lose their sense of wonder

Contents

Why Nature Games?—An Introduction

How games can awaken a child's sense of wonder and restore his kinship with his natural environment 9

Part I Sense-able Games 14

CHAPTER 1.   What Do You See?

Thirty-two activities and games which: require alert, quick, accurate observation—test visual perception and memory—suitably reward the winners—help children see the world as the animals do—encourage bird watching—require color identification —build a color vocabulary—point out design in nature—include designs children can make—demonstrate optical illusions—show nature's means of camouflage 15

CHAPTER 2.   What Do You Hear?

Twenty-seven activities and games which: require quick response to sound—are of both blindfold and open-eye type—investigate sound conduction—account for differences in pitch—involve listening to songs of birds and insects—build a hearing vocabulary 25

CHAPTER 3.   How Does It Feel?

Thirteen activities and games which: discuss touch as a safety device—show how the sense of touch can be fooled—pantomime physical reactions to things felt—show what organs animals feel with—build a touch vocabulary—require a discriminating sense of touch—involve blindfold identification of objects 32

CHAPTER 4.   How Does It Taste?

Sixteen activities and games which: connect taste with the other senses—demand blindfold taste identification—locate the various taste buds—pantomime reactions to tastes—build a taste vocabulary 36

CHAPTER 5.   How Does It Smell?

Fourteen activities and games which: discover how smells travel —require identification of objects by smell—ask children to describe how things smell—follow a scent—keep lists of different smells—pantomime reactions to smells—require boys and girls to smell objects before they see them 39

Part II Can You Name It? 42

CHAPTER 6.   Nature Name Games

Twenty-four games which: study the built-in transportation systems of seeds—identify the edible parts of plants—build a food vocabulary—increase children's familiarity with names of trees, birds, animals, etc.—include charades—help children learn about animals through their pets 43

CHAPTER 7.   Nature Quizzes

Twenty-three quizzes which: demand use of the exact words for animal groups, sexes, young, etc.—cover animal anatomy and evolution—raise thought-provoking questions—study nature under a microscope—sift fact from superstition—raise questions that can be answered by looking—include true-false questions—provide fun with riddles and puns 49

Part III Make It and Play It 60

CHAPTER 8.   Find-Its

Twenty-one activities and games such as: jigsaw puzzle with flowers—matching up flowers with leaves—those using sticks, stones, vegetables, etc. as playing materials—those requiring keen observation—making animals from twigs—nature collage—collecting games—making acorn people and walnut mice 61

CHAPTER 9.   Make-Its

Seventeen activities and games of chance and skill including: nine-men's morris—making and decorating javelins and friendship sticks—making a bird caller—making a whistle with a rubber band 67

CHAPTER 10.   Play-Its

Eighteen games of chance and skill including: puzzles galore—fox and geese—games requiring spatial conceptualization 74

Part IV Finders-Keepers 86

CHAPTER 11.   Treasure Hunts

Planning suggestions for seven hunts which: employ maps and clues—make youngsters think for themselves—stress accurate observation—provide suitable rewards 87

CHAPTER 12.   Scavenger Hunts

More than a dozen ideas for hunts which: stress social responsibility—impose time limits—include systems of point scoring 92

Part V   Shanks' Mares   96

CHAPTER 13.   Trips and Walks

Forty-six games which: require keen observation rather than
knowledge—explore unfamiliar areas—encourage the sharing of
pleasurable experiences—follow trails—stimulate the imagination
by dressing up natural objects—sharpen awareness of unusual
shapes—observe parasites—include fun-making stunts   97

Part VI   How Can You Tell?   106

CHAPTER 14.   The Weather

Sixteen ideas for quizzes and projects which include: distinguishing weather from climate—making weather vanes and anemome-
ters—measuring wind speed—learning U.S. Weather Bureau signals—making barometers—measuring rainfall and temperature—
using clouds as weather forecasters   107

CHAPTER 15.   The Sky

Ideas for over a dozen quizzes and projects which include: studying the solar system—showing how a sundial works—recording
the movements of stars and planets—interesting facts about the
planets—mapping the constellations—lists of planetariums and
observatories   114

Resources

Books and magazines containing: reference material—things children can make—games and activities—information on nature hobbies. Organizations supplying material on: camping—collecting—
safety—conservation   120

INDEX   125

Alphabetical index of games and activities—Index of games by type

Why Nature Games?

What *is* a game?

The very word, "game," shows its age and respectability. From the Anglo-Saxon "gamen," it has kept its original meaning— "sport; fun." Enjoyment is the basic ingredient.

What *is* nature? Do you have to be a Luther Burbank, or a John Burroughs, or a Rachel Carson to encourage children's interest in it?

Games can be building blocks or stepping stones to learning— without the pressures of school grades, homework, or school instruction. In this book, the term "game" is used to indicate any informal situation that appeals to the play instinct in the child. "Nature" is used just as loosely. The nature games are used here somewhat as spotlights—to single out simple, natural, interesting nature experiences to enjoy and find out about *together*.

There are hundreds of games that everybody can play—games in which laughter, curiosity, and sharing experiences are more important than a score. Games that *lead* somewhere; that awake a sense of wonder, interest, curiosity, "I wonder why . . . ?", "What if . . . ?", "Why does . . . ?"

Nature, too, is all around us—for those who see, hear, feel, taste, and touch. It's the pigeon on the city street, the pet dog, the flower in the windowbox, the icicle from the roof, the oil stain in the road, the rainbow in the sky.

It's the squish of mud between the toes, the taste of wild berries, the sound of a scolding squirrel, the feel of rough bark, a thorn, or a milkweed pod.

We sometimes forget that a child is *new*. Almost everything he does is a *first*: the first time he whistles; the first time he lights a fire; the first time he's blindfolded in a game; the first time he learns a new word, feels suspense, or enjoys applause. The first time he sees a butterfly, or snow; or tastes ice cream; or hears a bird sing; or feels the warm softness of a puppy.

Those firsts should be *fun*. They should lead on to seconds, and thirds, and on and on. They *will*, as long as that child keeps his sense of wonder.

Childhood, in this age of accelerated maturity, is growing shorter. Pressures are growing stronger. Children need periods of informal, relaxed play more than ever. They need simple, interesting games that provide exercise for growing muscles, stimulation for growing minds, and outlets for growing individualism. Games can do all this and more. Games can provide a contact, a bridge, to bring the child closer to the world of nature.

As the world shrinks, as production of food, shelter and clothing becomes more and more complex, the natural environment of the child shrinks, too. The supermarket replaces the raising and processing of farm and dairy products. The highways replace the country lanes. The bulldozer levels hills and trees.

A child's world is no longer bounded by home, school and church. The walls of the world are down. Today's child in the average home has seen a satellite being fired, has watched astronauts orbit and rendezvous in space. And that same child may never have seen a fish in a brook, a wren building her nest, or a spider web gleaming with dew in the early morning.

He has heard the sonic boom of a jet breaking the sound barrier, but he may never have heard the hooting of an owl at night, or the crowing of a cock at dawn. He has seen neon lights, but not a sunrise. He may have traveled far distances on planes and in cars, but never straddled a horse, or hiked a mountain trail.

He has eaten slices of watermelon on a hot day and has bought a pumpkin at Halloween, but he may never have seen a watermelon or pumpkin on the vine. He may never have shelled peas or shucked an ear of corn, seen a beehive, smelled pine needles, nibbled a sassafras twig, held a frog in his hands, built a fire, or slept overnight in a tent.

He can see an elephant in a zoo, but he may never have seen a live mouse. He can study a wildlife diorama of stuffed animals in a museum, but he may never have stroked the soft ears of a live rabbit. The city child who sees the heavens from an easy chair at the planetarium may never have lain on his back on a blanket on a hill and watched the warm starry sky of a summer night. The backyard grill has replaced the mystery of the open campfire.

The feeling of being part of the earth, at home in its natural surroundings, responsible for and interested in its conservation and preservation, can die out, unless, like Tinker Bell in Peter Pan, it is revived by love. This love of nature, this enjoyment, can be taught informally, through the use of the right games.

And that's where we can help—by making nature fun. And that's not hard. It doesn't take an expert. All it needs is an unhurried approach, a respect for the child as a person and a child's-eye look around at all the possibilities nearby.

If we are *aware* of the simple wonders around us, and if we share this awareness, we can help the child develop one of his greatest gifts—this gift of wonder. It's not important that we know all the right answers. Raising the right questions at the right time, in the right place, with the right child *is* important.

VIRGINIA W. MUSSELMAN

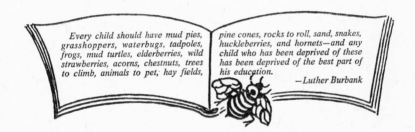

Every child should have mud pies, grasshoppers, waterbugs, tadpoles, frogs, mud turtles, elderberries, wild strawberries, acorns, chestnuts, trees to climb, animals to pet, hay fields, pine cones, rocks to roll, sand, snakes, huckleberries, and hornets—and any child who has been deprived of these has been deprived of the best part of his education.

—Luther Burbank

Acknowledgments

My thanks to Joseph Prendergast, Executive Vice President and Secretary of the National Recreation and Park Association and to James Rietmulder, Executive Vice President of Stackpole Books, for pushing me into writing this book.

My thanks to a mother with a very green thumb and a very big heart, full of love for all the world and its wonders.

My thanks to all the nature leaders whose games and activities have been distributed so widely and so generously that their very sources are now unknown. I wish they could all be credited individually.

Finally, to Erica Stiefel, friend, critic and secretary, my appreciation and thanks for her interest, her help and her attention to detail that kept the wheels of my department running smoothly while this book was in preparation.

Part I

Go out, keep your eyes open, your ears cocked, your nose sniffing, your hands free, your mouth shut and your feet dry!

- Marie Gaudette

Part One—Sense-able Games

Can you

SEE — — — — — — — — — —not just look?
LISTEN — — — — — — — — —not just hear?
FEEL — — — — — — — — — —not just touch?
TASTE — — — — — — — —not just swallow?
SMELL — — — — — — — —not just sniff?

CHILDREN can—when someone shows them how. Children *will*—when someone makes it fun to do.

Learning to use the five senses is the key that opens the doors to the wonders of the world. Maybe that key has grown a bit rusty for lack of use by us, but soon it will get shinier than ever when a child is at that door, waiting for someone to turn that key. Take him by the hand and go with him into the world of Nature.

That World is EVERYWHERE

That Someone is YOU

That Child is ANY CHILD

CHAPTER 1

What Do You See?

Nothing but city cement and asphalt? Nothing but sand on a beach? Rocks on a mountain? Grass in a meadow? Trees in the woods?

Look again. Take time to SEE.

What about sun, rain, stars, clouds, earth, water, moon?

What about leaves, flowers, birds, animals, people?

What about COLORS of things?

What about SHAPES of things?

What about SIZES of things?

What about WORDS for all of these?

Curiosity can be the first step toward observation. Observation leads to wonder. Wonder goes straight into appreciation and from there comes life-long enjoyment of the marvelous world of nature and all its creatures.

Games that require observation help the child to learn how to use and to enjoy his sense of sight. Impossible? All it takes is TIME to look, compare, analyze, discover, and discuss, plus somebody to share those discoveries—somebody who puts them into a child's pattern of learning through play.

GAME LEAD-UPS FOR THE EYES

Games that encourage SEEING can be lead-ups to games that encourage seeing the world of nature. Be sure to take that next step. Don't stop with these—they're just warm-ups—just interest-arousers.

Statues ✓

One child is It, and stands facing a tree, post, house, or other place. The others stand behind a starting line. It counts to ten as quickly or as slowly as he wishes. The others advance as far as they dare. Then It turns quickly. If he sees anyone in motion, he calls him by name, and that person must go back to the starting line.

The game goes on until some or all of the players are close to It. While his back is turned, one brave child dares to tap him and everybody dashes for the starting line, It in hot pursuit. Whoever is caught is the next It.

This is a favorite game—full of suspense, argument and excitement. Each child will complain and argue over every decision It makes—and love it. It must use his eyes to spot any movement. The players use their eyes to watch It and to decide when it is safe to move.

Variation: It is blindfolded, and must try to *hear* any movements.

Find the Leader ✓

It hides his eyes or leaves the area while the others select a leader. When It removes the blindfold or comes back, all the others are making some motion selected by a chosen leader, such as waving the right hand. Every now and then the leader changes the motion and the others also quickly change to the new one. It tries to catch this change of movement, and so find out who the leader is. When he does, they change places.

Sharp Eyes

The youngsters form two teams, facing each other about four or five feet apart. At a signal, each person looks carefully at the player opposite him. At another signal, both lines turn around so they face in opposite directions.

Each person then alters two items in his appearance—unties a shoelace, unfastens a button, takes off his shoes, changes his hair some way, takes off glasses, etc.

At the third signal, the two lines turn to face each other again, and each child tries to spot the changes of the person opposite. Team with the greatest number of correct answers wins.

I Spy

Hide some small object (pebble, pinecone, etc.) in plain sight, but where it is not obvious. Everybody looks for it. When someone sees it, he must not show that he has found it, but must come over and report to the scorekeeper.

Variation: Hide a number of small items where they are in full sight, but hard to see, such as a twig on the ground under a tree, a piece of grass on grass, a white clover near white daisies, a brown acorn on the brown earth, etc. Make a list of such items. Each child comes over and reports what he has noticed. First to report all the objects is Mr. Keen-Eye Spy.

Eye-Openers

How well can the youngsters visualize? Fifteen items to answer with pencil and paper. Think back.

1. When a horse lies down, which end of him gets up first?	Front
2. Which end of a dog gets up first?	Either
3. Which end of a cat gets up first?	Either
4. Which end of a man gets up first?	Head
5. Does a cow trot?	No
6. With which hand does the Statue of Liberty hold her torch?	Right
7. What does she hold in her other hand?	A book
8. On which side does a policeman wear his badge?	Left
9. How many wheels has a freight car?	Eight
10. Which is larger, a dime or a cent?	Cent
11. Whose picture is printed on a dollar greenback?	Washington's
12. Did Abe Lincoln part his hair in the middle?	No
13. When we chew, does the upper jaw move?	No
14. Do the funnels of a ship lean forward or backward?	Backward
15. How many keys are there on an ordinary piano?	88

Next time—take more notice!

When the arguments over these questions are all over, each child may like to think up his own questions to ask the others, the answers of which are based on past observation.

Guess-Whats

Without looking—just *thinking*—everybody writes down his guesses and tests his perceptual memory.

1. What is the diameter of a penny? A dime? A nickel? A quarter? A half-dollar?
2. How long is a dollar bill? How wide?
3. How long is the handle of the average broom or mop?
4. What is the size of the average airmail stamp?
5. How large is the bottom of a telephone? The mouthpiece?
6. What is the height of the seat of the average dining room chair?

Finished guessing? Take a ruler, or tape measure, and find the right answers. (Good training in measuring, too.)

Penny-Wise

Everybody looks at an ordinary Lincoln penny, and tries to find

What our forefathers fought for	Liberty
Part of a hill	Brow
Name of a song	America
You and I together	US
Part of an Indian weapon	Bow
Part of Indian corn	Ear

Who's Your Friend? √

Hang a sheet, blanket, or large piece of newspaper over a doorway, clothesline or tree limb, in such a way that a small slit or opening can be used. The youngsters take turns being the audience, trying to guess the identity of the others by: first, their noses; second, their hands; third, their feet.

The others hide behind the blanket. One at a time, each sticks his nose in the slit. When those in the audience have finished trying to guess the owners of the noses, each backstager takes a turn sticking his hand through the slit. Finally, each in turn sticks a foot under the blanket.

The person in the audience making the most correct identifications gets a Super-I-Spy badge or star, made out of tinfoil or aluminum foil.

Memory Test

Test the visual memory of the boys and girls.

Place ten different objects in a paper bag. Take them out one at a time, hold them up for a few seconds, and replace them in the bag. Then ask each youngster to list the objects he saw *in the order in which they were shown.* Use simple objects such as a pine cone, acorn, pebble, burr, leaf, flowers, twig, berry, seedpod, etc.—things easy to find locally.

Variation: Use all vegetables. All fruits. All flowers. Instead of a bag, put the items on a tray. Give each person a quick look, then cover the tray. Then see how many objects they can remember and name.

Right Whites

Prepare eight or more small jars of white food staples used in cooking. Label each jar with a number but no name. Each person tries to identify the contents of each jar by sight alone.

Staples might include:

salt	white cornmeal	powdered milk
sugar	baking powder	dehydrated mashed potatoes
flour	baking soda	cream of tartar

This sort of guessing game can be played with other colors, other foods, such as spices and seasonings—any items that encourage observation.

NATURE LOOK-SEES

Bug's-Eye View

Everyone stretches out, eyes on grass level, to see what the world is like to a bug. The blade of grass is like a tree! The pebble is mountain-size—to a bug. Big things like trees just don't show. People are just feet.

Bird's-Eye View

Visit a lookout tower, church steeple, fire tower, roof of a high building, or top of a high hill or mountain and see what the world looks like to a bird. Big things look small. Small things disappear.

Fish-Eye View

At the pool, beach, pond or lake, look at the world from the water level. What can a fish see?

Child's View

Ever wonder why a child is unimpressed by a large building, or is frightened by unfamiliar adults? Get down on the floor and see the world childwise. Adults are legs. Tables are houses. Chair legs are posts.

Bird Tree

Find a big, bare branch or stick and hang it in some prominent place. Every time anyone sees a new bird, he draws it on cardboard, colors it with crayons, initials it as his, and ties it on the bird tree.

How many new birds can be spotted in a week? Birds have names. Look them up in a bird book. Learn their names. It's more fun to say "cardinal," than just "red bird."

Learn their shapes, too, and the way they fly.
Who's the best birder?

Flight Watch

Go with the youngsters to a quiet place, sit quietly, and watch the flight of birds. Try to see birds that

- soar like gliders
- flap their wings steadily
- fly up and down in short curves
- make very short flights
- fly very high
- fly very low
- sing, whistle or make other sounds in flight.

Do birds take off or land against the wind, or with the wind? Can a bird fly backwards?

Why don't birds fall off their perches when they're asleep? Look at a pet canary or parakeet and find out.

COLOR

The ability to recognize and identify colors can be learned, and the learning can be fun. Learning the exact shade is even more fun, and word-building, too. Encourage a wide color vocabulary by showing color charts. Paint shops are a good source.

I See a Color

One child looks around the area and selects some object in sight. He says, "I see something blue," or whatever color the object is. The others take turns trying to guess it. The first to guess correctly chooses the next object to be guessed.

Variation: To make this a bit harder and more interesting even for young children, add more dialogue, so that It and the others must be even more observant.

It says, "From where I sit (or stand) I see something blue" (or other color). The next person says, "Is it . . . ?", naming something *he* sees that is blue. It answers truthfully, "No, it's not. . . ." Player # 3 suggests something else that is blue, and the game goes on until someone asks about the right object. He then becomes It.

This game is a sort of visual treasure hunt. Children always enjoy it. It's a good game, too, because it requires observation plus color identification.

Color Tours

A walk around any area—backyard or city block, camp or playground—can promote observation and color identification. These are only a few of the many variations:

1. See how many *red* objects can be spotted—any shade of red. Same with other colors, on other color tours. Make a list along the way.

2. See how many *different* colors can be spotted. Make a list.
3. Follow 1 and 2, but don't make a list. See how many can be *remembered* and named after getting back to the starting point.
4. Keep personal progress trends. It's how well the person observes, not the number of items somebody else saw.

Color Wheel ✓

Find a sample of a color wheel in an art store or book. Draw a big one on a large piece of cardboard, and color it.

Then take the group out to find natural objects that match the colors on the wheel, bring them back, and match them up. It may take a long time to fill some of the color sections, but it is fun to work on it.

Color Family

The youngsters see how many names they can think up for any color. How many words meaning red? Or green? Blue? Yellow? Black?

They take turns naming a word that describes one color (such as pink, rose, scarlet, crimson, etc.). When somebody misses, he gets a point against him. Five points and he pays some sort of forfeit.

They take turns naming items such as flowers, fruits, birds, etc., of special colors. It says "Red!" and points to someone. That person must answer by giving the name of something red before It can count to ten.

Color Trickery

On a large sheet of paper, ask the youngsters to draw a U. S. flag and crayon it heavily. Make the stripes green and black, the stars (all fifty of them!) orange. Then, hang it in a bright room.

Ask each person to stare at it fixedly for several minutes, then look at a bare wall. There's the flag—the way it *ought* to look, all red, white and blue!

DESIGN

The world of nature is full of all sorts of shapes and designs. No two snowflakes are alike, even though every single one has the same number of sides—six. Take a magnifying glass, catch a few snow flakes on a dark surface and let the youngsters see the variety!

LOOK for designs:

leaves against the sky
bare tree limbs in the winter
bird shapes and silhouettes
color swirls in an oilslick
color lines in a feather
drifts of snow or sand
bark on a tree
spider web

curve of a butterfly's wing
op art on a caterpillar
erosion rings on a pebble
swirl lines on a seashell
peas in a pod
cloud formations
ripples on water

MAKE designs the play way:

String-Alongs

Provide construction paper, and jars of tempera paint in various colors.

Each child takes a piece of heavy string or yarn about 36″ long, dips it into whatever color he likes, lets it drip a moment or so, then lays it bit by bit on the paper in any design he makes up as he goes along. When the string is in place, he takes a paper towel and presses it over the string—a heavy press for a heavy line, a light press for a light line.

If he likes, he can dip another string into another color, place it on the paper, and continue making designs until the string print pleases him.

Huff and Puff Designs

Shelf paper is good for this, because the paper shouldn't be too absorbent.

Near the bottom of the paper, the child drops a blob of paint. Then he takes a drinking straw and without touching the paint, blows it around the paper in any design he likes. The first attempt is likely to look like a tree or plant, especially if a dark color was used. Smaller blobs of brighter color can be blown around it so as to look like flowers.

As the child learns how to handle the colors and the straw, the designs will take bolder and more original forms. Balance and interesting color combinations will begin to show up.

EYES RIGHT—OR WRONG?

The eyes can be fooled. Television often uses trick photography. Magicians mystify by their sleight of hand that isn't seen because the other hand and the magician's talk have distracted the eyes of his audience. Nature is full of camouflage, too.

Op Art

Sight can be tricky. Straight lines, circles, divisions of light and shadow can lead the eye to draw incorrect conclusions as to length, width, size, shape and weight. Op art (optical art) is based on such principles. Let the youngsters look for examples.

Look down a railroad track, or a highway with fences on each side. The tracks and the fences don't really meet in the distance, but the eyes see them meeting in a long V.

Throw a stone into a pond. The eyes will follow the widening circles until they're lost at the shoreline.

Create a vortex by stirring a pail of water vigorously in one direction. The eyes will follow that conelike "hole" in the water to its very bottom.

Triple Sight

Find two small cards, visiting cards are just right. On one of them prick three small holes close together, in the form of a triangle. On the other card, prick just one hole. Then hold the card with the three holes as close to the eye as possible, and hold the other card about two or three inches in front of the first. Look toward a light, and your eye will tell you that both cards have three holes! You can't always believe what you see!

Disappearing Dime

Put a dime in an ordinary drinking cup or glass. Then ask one person to back away from the cup and lower his head until the edge of the cup hides the dime. He holds that position. Pour water slowly into the cup—and presto! The dime comes into sight!

Why? Water bends light. The light gets reflected from the dime around the edge of the cup to the child's eye, so that he sees the dime. Experiment with underwater objects in the pool. Are they where they should be? Why is it so hard to pick them up? Why is it hard to net or spear a fish?

Camouflage

Protective coloring often keeps us from seeing something in plain sight. Look for examples of it. The grass snake, the garter snake, the frog, the ground-feeding birds like the thrush, the sparrows, the partridge and grouse; the trout in the brook; birds' nests; caterpillars. Do they blend into their background? What was the background? Look, next time! Keep a list. Talk about nature's hide-aways. Every section of the country has its own examples of nature's camouflage.

Why are animals camouflaged? Is there just one reason? Or

are there several? Is the same reason true for all? Can you find any animal homes that are camouflaged?

Protective coloring is used by people too. Why do some hunters wear bright caps? Why do some hunters wear brownish or gray clothes? Why are life preservers usually white or bright yellow? Why do jungle fighters stick grass and twigs in their helmets?

Does *movement* have anything to do with protective coloring? Watch a grasshopper, or a butterfly, a spider, "walking stick," or squirrel. Did you see it before it moved?

CHAPTER 2

What Do You Hear?

Hearing, like the sense of sight, has a very definite relationship with the enjoyment and appreciation of nature.

The high noise level of modern living—traffic, jets, building construction, radio, television—is more likely to teach a child to "turn off" his hearing than to develop and enjoy it.

Sounds are all around us, if we listen. The sounds of music, waves, winds, voices, food cooking, birds singing, dogs barking, footsteps, balls bouncing, bells ringing, leaves rustling, boys whistling—are everyday sounds, but adding color and excitement to living.

Often sight is given more attention than hearing, but the *total impression* needs both. One reinforces the other. Only the blind and the deaf realize how limited the sense of hearing or seeing can be without the other.

Learning to hear and to distinguish the sounds around him is a skill that the child can use all his life. It's a useful skill, too, because his alertness in hearing and analyzing sounds will contribute specifically to his school life and to his physical safety, as well as to his appreciation of nature's sounds.

This alertness, this quick response to hearing, can be cultivated. Games that require such quick response, or demand a concentration on listening, are excellent tools for this training.

LEAD-UP GAMES TO ENCOURAGE LISTENING

Blindfold Games

They're full of suspense. They encourage daring. They're dramatic. They demand alertness and concentration on listening. Keep them safe by setting up a special play area. Use paper bags for masks. (More sanitary—and safer for the smallies because a bit of ground can be seen.) Here are several games. Follow them with others, and make up variations.

French Blindman's Buff

Full of suspense, and quick thinking. The youngsters move

around in a circle, with the Frenchman blindfolded in the center. He has a cane or stick. When he is ready, he taps his cane on the ground, and everyone in the circle must stand still. He points the cane at somebody. This person must come forward, take hold of the end of the cane, and answer any questions he wants to ask. He has three guesses in trying to identify the voice. If he guesses right, they change places. If wrong, the game starts again.

Jingling Match

A very old English game like blindman's buff. Only everybody *except* It is blindfolded. It carries a bell or bunch of keys to let the others know where he is. The one who catches him becomes the next It. Play this in a definite, limited space.

Bow-Wow

One person sits in the middle of a circle, blindfolded, a ball or rock or other object within arm's length. Each player, one at a time, tries to creep up without making a sound, and take the ball. If he makes it safely, everyone claps, and *he* becomes the Bow-Wow. If Bow-Wow hears a child, he barks "Bow Wow!" and somebody else takes a turn at trying to move noiselessly.

Variation: Call this game "Indian Scout." The Indian gives a war whoop if he hears anyone approach him. Good for letting off steam!

Shake the Keys

Choose It; blindfold him. He stands in the center of the circle. Pass a bunch of keys around *quietly* from person to person. The keys go around until somebody decides to shake the keys. It must try to point directly to the one who shook the keys. If he guesses correctly, he trades places with that player.

Snatch the Keys

Choose It again and blindfold him. He sits in the center of the circle with the keys in front of him. One at a time, the others try to sneak the keys without being heard by It. If It hears the keys, he trades places with the player who jingled them. (No keys? Use baby rattle, bells, pebbles in a tin can.)

Deer Stalking

A very successful and exciting game, depending upon silence for its suspense.

One person is the Deer, another the Hunter. Each is blindfolded and placed at opposite ends of a large table (pingpong

26

table is good). The Hunter must try to catch the Deer, and the Deer tries to avoid being caught. Neither can go beyond touch of the table, and neither should make a sound.

The others watch in complete silence; no laughing or whispering. If the Deer and Hunter can go barefoot, it's even better.

Harness Race

Play in couples. One person is the horse, the other the rider. The horse wears a clothesline halter and is blindfolded. On the track between the starting line and the goal are several narrow strips of cardboard. These are hurdles over which the horse must jump. The rider guides the horse with the harness, and with spoken directions. If the horse steps on any of the hurdles, he must return and try again. The rider may not touch the horse. All directions must be given by voice and halter.

Still Pond, No More Moving

It is blindfolded and spun around to confuse his sense of direction. The others scatter within a playing area. They move around freely until It calls out "Still pond, no more moving!" At those words, all the children must stay where they are, except that they are allowed three steps if needed. It then gropes around, trying to find someone. If and when he does, he has to guess whom he has caught. If he guesses right, that person becomes It. If not right, he tries again.

Adaptation: It calls out "Still pond, no more moving," and everyone stays in place. Then It gives them any leeway he wishes, such as "Take a hop, two steps and a jump." When each player has followed instructions, the game goes on as usual, with It trying to find a victim.

This game goes on and on, because it's exciting and full of suspense.

Blindman's Cane

Like French blindman's buff, but funnier and more difficult.

The youngsters form a circle around It, who is blindfolded and holds a cane or stick in his hand. They circle around until It calls "Stop!" He then points his cane toward where he thinks somebody may be standing. If he's right, that person must go up and take the end of It's cane. It then asks him to growl like a dog, or roar like a lion, or make some other animal sound, while It tries to identify him by that sound. If It guesses right, the other person takes his place.

If It guesses wrong, the players circle around again and the game goes on.

Ducky Lucky

A funny, happy little game depending upon voice identification.

One person is blindfolded and given a pillow or cushion. The others sit in a circle, on chairs, or on the ground.

It puts his cushion on somebody's lap and says, "Ducky Lucky!" That person must answer by saying "Quack, Quack!" It then tries to guess who the player is. He may ask for a few other sounds, such as "Bark like a dog," or "Crow like a rooster." If he guesses right, the other person becomes Ducky Lucky.

Stalking

A really exciting game, full of suspense. Set aside an open area, indoor or outdoor, around 40' x 60' if possible. Mark a center line across it, a starting line at one end and a finish line at the other. Station three blindfolded sentries along the center line.

At a signal, a group of youngsters (the stalkers) stealthily start toward the finish line trying to pass the sentries without being heard. The sentries try to detect the stalkers, and point at them. When judges, stationed along the sidelines, see a sentry point out a stalker, they signal the stalker to sit down where he is.

The game is over when all the stalkers have been detected, or have successfully reached the finish line. Stalkers must stay in place until the sentries have removed their blindfolds, so that they may see how successful they were in detecting the sounds of the stalkers. Sidelines must keep absolutely still.

Variation 1: Station a sentry in the middle of a wood road or path.

Variation 2: Play in a circle. Sentry in the center. Stalker must creep up from edge of circle and touch the sentry without being heard.

Open-eye Hearing Games

Bell Ringer

Find a barrel hoop, make a hoop out of heavy cardboard, or use an old tire. Decorate it; it's more fun that way. Hang a small bell by a string so that it dangles in the center of the hoop. Then hang the hoop from a tree limb, clothesline or other place, just so the hoop and the bell hang free.

Each person gets five "shots" at the hoop, and tries to throw a beanbag, pinecone, small ball or other object through the hoop in such a way as to make the bell ring. The one with the highest score wins.

Variation: Play this game blindfolded; score when bell rings.

Birds Fly

An old game always popular because it demands a quick response to hearing.

Everybody stands informally, at arm's length from one another. It tries to fool them by naming not only objects that fly, but also those that don't fly. Players must flap their arms every time a flying object is named, such as "Geese fly," "Planes fly," etc. They must *not* flap their arms when It calls "Dogs fly," "Pigs fly," etc., even though It flaps his arms and tries to fool them into imitating him.

Sound Dropping

From behind a sheet or curtain, or in another room, drop a series of objects. The children try to identify each by the sound. Use:

coin	tin cup	log	cane
apple	lemon	rock	shoe

NATURE LISTENERS

Sound Waves

What *is* sound? How does it carry? It's fun to find out.

Tie a piece of string around the middle of a poker or other metal rod, so that the poker hangs down in front of the child. He holds the two ends of the string to his ears. Strike the poker very lightly with a piece of metal (nail, for example). He'll hear a loud, booming sound, but anyone nearby will hear only a small sound.

Find a long, flat board. One person puts his ear flat against it at one end. If another person scratches the wood gently at the other end, the sound will be carried down to the listening ear. When the listener's eyes are shut, place a watch on the other end and see if he can hear the ticking.

Try this on the ground, like the Indians. One person kneels and puts his ear to the ground. The others tramp in place, some distance away. Experiment to find out how far away they can be and still be heard.

Look at different kinds of ears. Has the shape anything to do with hearing? Why does a dog cock his ears? Why does a person sometimes put a hand behind his ear to try to hear better?

Experiment with different sounds. Tap different parts of the body; objects like chairs, tables, walls, poles, windows. Are they all alike or different?

Make a drum and a rattle. Experiment with *beat*.

What about *pitch?* Does the length of a wire or rubber band have anything to do with whether the tone is high or low?

Pour a different amount of water in several glasses, and tap them with a stick or spoon. Experiment with the amount of water in each until the different tones can make a tune.

Whistling Contest
One of the first sound skills that boys and girls learn is whistling. They can learn to *listen* to how they sound, by these simple contests:

- longest whistle with one breath
- best tune of a required song
- best duet
- longest whistling without smiling
- loudest whistle, with and without fingers
- best imitation of a barnyard fowl or animal
- best imitation of any well-known bird
- greatest number of bird songs

Encourage practice on the last two items. Use the bird songs from Cornell University, and whistle along with them. Trying to imitate a sound is a good way to remember it.

Write to Cornell University Records, Cornell University Press, 124 Roberts Place, Ithaca, New York for its catalogue. It will list the records best suited for the different sections of the United States: Western Birds; Florida Birds; Birds of the North Woods; Southern Woods and Gardens; American Game Birds, and many more, including Birds of Africa, and of Mexico.

Youngsters will enjoy the records of the Songs of Insects, too. They'll be fascinated by the record on Voices of the Night, that gives the calls of thirty-four frogs and toads in the United States and Canada. They're available from the same source.

Use such records to show how wonderful and how diverse the sounds of nature can be.

Birds' Opera House

Somewhere in the garden or near the camp, or in the woods or park, there's a spot where birds like to sing. Try to find it. Then visit it quietly, in very small groups, and *listen*. Try to locate the birds by sight, too. Remember their shape, color, markings and song. Look them up in a bird book. Try to remember the songs by whistling them.

Listening Corner, Post, Tree or Lean-to

Find some quiet, out-of-the-way place. Visit it with just one or two youngsters. Sit down, stay still, and enjoy the sounds that you'd miss if you didn't listen.

Look, too, at the little things you wouldn't see if you weren't quiet—a leaf suddenly twisting, a bit of red-capped moss, a bird's nest almost hidden.

Touch the tree behind you and feel its bark. *Feel* the sun on your hand, the softness of moss, the dry feel of dead leaves.

Horizontal Club

Members go to the listening lean-to, lie down flat, look up, and *listen*.

Indian Hike

Go in single file, v-e-r-y carefully. Try not to make a *sound*. Avoid stepping on dry twigs or through dry leaves. Don't talk above a whisper. Stop frequently to *listen* as well as look. What sounds can be heard?

Listen for wind, song of a bird, rustle of some small animal, a distant plane, water running, leaves rustling, squirrel chattering, insect humming. Look for *sources* of all the sounds.

Hearing Vocabulary

Everybody tries to name as many words as possible that mean *loud*.

How many ways to describe the sound of a bell? The sound of the sea? The wind? Thunder? A voice? A footstep?

Keep a running list of all the words that describe a sound, and see how many can be added to daily use, instead of the usual "loud" or "quiet."

CHAPTER 3

How Does It Feel?

The sense of touch is another of the five senses that is often taken for granted, instead of being recognized as highly important, useful, very interesting, and a source of enjoyment. The blind child, reading by running his fingertips over the small indentations that make up the Braille language knows how important that sense of touch is.

Life would be very empty if we couldn't enjoy and use our sense of touch. We'd miss all the good "feels"—warmth, softness, smoothness, sharpness, cold, moisture. We'd miss the feel of textures—of sidewalks, floors, walls, furniture, fur, feathers, hair, leather, china, glass, tree trunks.

We'd miss the feel of the wind and sun, of earth under our feet, of snow, mud, sand, and water.

The sense of touch is a safety device, too. It gives warnings to the brain, so that we automatically stop, or draw back, or take other precautions to keep out of possible danger.

Think up and discuss situations when the sense of touch is a safety device, such as:

- drawing back when touching something too hot.
- walking gingerly when the floor is slippery.
- holding the hands out in front when walking in the dark.

Those are *voluntary* reactions. Nature helps us even more by providing *involuntary* reactions, too, such as:

- the eye watering when it feels a foreign object in it.
- the body coughing when it feels something caught in the throat, or when food or liquid "goes the wrong way."
- the adrenal gland pouring extra adrenalin in when we're in danger, must fly from it, or meet some physical challenge.

What others can the group think of and discuss?

Fooling Feel

The sense of touch, like sight, can be fooled. Try it!

Place a marble or other small round object on a table. Ask a youngster to cross his first and second fingers, and roll the marble back and forth with them. How many marbles can he *see*? One. How many can he *feel*? Two!

Ask him to rub his crossed first and second fingers up and down the bridge of his nose. He'll feel *two* noses!

Feelings

Youngsters pantomime their physical reactions when they feel:

ice-cold water at the beach	a splinter in the finger
something sticky	a sudden rain shower
snow getting in over their galoshes	a puppy or other soft animal
something that is too hot	warm blanket on a cold night
pebbles with bare feet	skis for the first time
electric fan on a hot day	

They select their own "feels" to pantomime, and take turns guessing.

Blind Game

Everybody is blindfolded. They take turns touching some object with one finger and trying to guess what it is. Use such objects as:

piece of bark	seedpod
vegetable	flowerhead
piece of fur	bird's nest
moss	animal
ice	soil

Weight-Guessing

Pass around several objects of various sizes and shapes. Each person "hefts" them, and writes down his guess as to the weight of each. Use objects such as:

watermelon	rocks	apples
cucumber	head of cabbage	bunch of grapes
a dog	a can	a child

Then bring out the scales and check each object.

Encourage the practice of weight-guessing. It's good training for the senses.

Animal Feelers

Watch a cat wash its whiskers. What are whiskers for? Do mice have whiskers? Why? Do whiskers work like a small alarm system? Whiskers would be useful in what sort of emergency?

Look at a butterfly's feelers through a magnifying glass. What are they like?

Do ants have feelers? Look and see.

Watch a daddy longlegs walk along. What happens when one leg touches some obstacle?

Verbalizing Touch

The youngsters think up all the words possible that describe how things *feel,* such as:

crisp	sharp	furry	soft	wet	cold
oily	heavy	light	feathery	dry	warm
smooth	rough	ridged	slippery	hot	damp
round	carved	scaly	flaky	mushy	rubbery

They think up as many *objects* as possible that fit these words, like "crisp crackers" or "crisp curtains" or "crisp weather."

They keep a running list of words that describe how things *feel,* and try to use them in everyday talk.

Grab Bag

Collect about fifteen articles, such as a pinecone, acorn, piece of bark, moss, pebble, shell, feather, milkweed pod, burr, etc. Put each in a small plastic bag. Pass the bags around quickly to the blindfolded youngsters until everybody has had a fast feel. Then each person tries to list as many articles as he can. Longest listing wins.

Variation: Place all the objects in one plastic bag, and pass it around the circle. Each person may take only a very quick feel; then everyone writes down as many objects as he can identify and remember.

√ Finger Memory

Blindfold one player. The others move around It until he calls "Come closer, friends!" Then they all come close, and try to touch It without being caught. When someone is caught, It must identify him by touching his face and head. If It guesses correctly, that person becomes the new It.

(This game is played all over the world, with different names, but with the same excitement of touch identification.)

Finger Identification

Collect a boxful of nature's odds and ends—leaves, seeds,

34

burrs, grasses, flowers, acorns, nuts, pinecones, twigs, pebbles, shells, and the like—things common to your area.

Each child in turn is blindfolded. He goes through the contents of the box, making piles of all similar objects—all the acorns together, all pebbles together, etc. He is timed, and his time recorded. The one with the most accurate and fastest sense of touch wins.

This game is worth practicing. It teaches concentration as well as touch identification.

Tricky Touch

The sense of touch can be fooled, just as the other senses can. Stick two thumbtacks through a piece of thin cardboard so that the points are about a half-inch apart. Blindfold a child, and press the points lightly against one of his fingertips. He'll feel both thumbtacks, because the fingertips are sensitive.

Then press the tacks to the back of his neck. He'll probably feel only one, because that area of the body is not so sensitive as the fingertips.

Try this on other parts of the body. (This trick works best if the person doesn't *see* the thumbtacked cardboard, but just reports on what he *felt*.

Try other experiments. Does heat make the skin more sensitive? Cold? How does a piece of ice feel when it is held to the skin too long? If blindfolded, does the child think he's being burned? That's an old initiation trick.

Tell the child that you can press a penny to his forehead so hard that he won't be able to shake it off. Press it hard, but take it off again by having your forefinger wet. He will continue to feel it, and will shake and shake his head until he decides he's being fooled.

CHAPTER 4

How Does It Taste?

Our sense of taste is responsible for the pleasure we get out of food and drink. It varies with different persons. It can be cultivated by *thinking* about how things taste, and taking time to enjoy the sensations of eating or drinking things we enjoy.

It can be dulled, too, by lack of conscious use, by poor eating habits, such as too many very hot foods, or too many cold drinks, or smoking, etc.

It is closely tied in with all the other senses. Just think about that.

Don't crunchy apples and celery *sound* good?

Don't some foods *look* good, like brown pancakes, or red tomatoes, or ripe peaches?

Don't foods *smell* good? Like bacon cooking, or hot popcorn, or cinnamon toast?

Don't some foods *feel* good, like the texture of ice cream, and juicy pears?

Very often, it's the way food *looks,* or *smells,* or *sounds,* or *feels* that helps us to decide that it tastes good and we like it, or it doesn't taste good and we don't like it.

Talk about favorite foods. What is it especially about each that makes it so good?

Talk about *un*-favorite foods. What is there about each that makes it *not* taste good?

Prove how closely the senses of sight, smell and taste work together. Here's one way. It's interesting.

Blind Taster

Blindfold someone, and ask him to hold his nose tightly so that he can't smell. Then give him a bite of something with a distinctive *smell*, like a small piece of chocolate bar. He probably won't be able to identify it. (That's why it's a good idea to hold the nose when swallowing a bad-tasting medicine!)

Where Is Taste?

Find out!

Dissolve a spoonful of sugar in half a glass of water. Dip a toothpick in it, and touch the toothpick lightly to different parts of a child's tongue. Where did it taste sweetest?

Try the same experiment with salt; then with vinegar; then with an aspirin dissolved in water.

The tastebuds for sugar are on the tip of the tongue. For salt, the tip and sides. For vinegar, the sides. For aspirin, the back of the tongue.

Tastings

Get the youngsters to pantomime their physical reactions to tasting something that is

too hot	very peppery
too cold	oily
too bitter	very sweet
very good	very sour
something distasteful	something unfamiliar

Verbalizing Taste

The youngsters think up all the words possible that describe how anything *tastes,* like:

fresh	fishy	burned	pungent
sweet	sour	bitter	nutty
bland	salty	spicy	oily

Everybody figures out how many of those words describe *smell,* too.

Then they try to name as many foods as possible that could be described by each word.

Everyone *uses* the descriptive words. Look up the meaning of any unfamiliar ones.

Everybody describes the taste of as many vegetables as possible:

potatoes	onions	carrots
beets	cabbage	spinach
asparagus	celery	leeks
tomatoes	broccoli	turnips
parsnips	cauliflower	green peppers
peas	beans	corn

They pretend they are talking to somebody who has never

heard of any of those vegetables, and try to describe them in terms of taste, touch, smell, texture, and sound.

Everybody listens to such a description and then draws the way he thinks that vegetable would look if he didn't know how it really looked!

Play the same games, using fruits instead of vegetables.

strawberries	apples	pears
peaches	blueberries	raspberries
plums	cherries	bananas
pineapple	watermelon	cantaloupe

How many edible *wild* foods have they ever found and tasted?

wild grapes	blackberries
dandelion greens	groundnuts
blueberries	hickory nuts
persimmons	mushrooms

How many edible *seeds* can they name, and have they tasted in bread or cereal?

wheat	rye	corn
rice	oats	barley

CHAPTER 5

How Does It Smell?

It is said that the sense of smell can trigger the memory quicker and for a longer time than any of the other senses. We may forget names, faces and places, but a smell of baking bread, or lilacs in the spring, will bring back scenes and events that had been forgotten for years.

Sometimes we neglect our sense of smell, ignore it unless the smell is very strong, very pleasant, or very unpleasant.

What Is Smell?

Why is the coffee can, or the perfume bottle, or the spice jar kept carefully covered? How far do the molecules that carry the smell spread out? Experiment and see.

Put some ground coffee in a shallow saucer. The youngsters come near it slowly. Find out how far away it can be smelled. Leave it an hour and then let them measure the distance again. Is it the same? Or have all the molecules carrying the smell left the coffee?

Sniffer Quiz

Place items that have distinctive odors in tightly covered cans or jars, numbering each. Cover each so that the contents can't be seen, and no name is visible. Number each for identification.

Youngsters take turns smelling the contents of each, and then write down their guesses. The contents might include small amounts of such items as:

coffee	tea leaves	cheese	cinnamon
lemon	lime	chocolate	mustard
nutmeg	bay leaf	sage	garlic
onion	oil of wintergreen	leather	soap
vanilla	vinegar	mint	grapes

Using the same items, the youngsters try to find the word that most exactly describes the smell of each.

Each person thinks carefully and then tells what event in his life each of the following smells makes him think of:

smoke	gasoline fumes	tar
fish	sweat	perfume
fresh-cut grass	meat broiling	talcum powder
hay	bacon cooking	kerosene

Everybody thinks up and makes a list of all the words that can be used to describe how something smells. Try to use them all in the course of a week.

How many of those words can also describe *taste*?

Each person tries to remember the very first time he ever smelled those special odors. How old was he? Where was he? What was he doing?

Each person pantomimes his favorite smell, for the others to try to guess.

Everybody decides upon and talks about what he thinks is the nicest smell in the world.

Onion Hunt

One person (or chosen leader) lays out a trail a few minutes before the others follow. He rubs a fresh-cut onion across tree trunks, telephone poles, walls, or other places. The others must "follow their noses." Keep this hunt short, so that the smell of the onion won't disappear too soon.

Nosey Walk

Take the youngsters on a walk around the block, playground, park, or camp, and see how many different smells can be identified.

Keep a list, and add new smells as they are identified. Keep several lists: home smells, camp smells, street smells, playground smells, garden smells.

Act-a-Smell

Each person pantomimes his physical reaction to some special smell. Others try to guess what it is.

Outdoor Smelling

Everybody keeps a count of the number of objects that he smells *before* he sees them. Possibilities like:

new-cut grass	ocean beach	tar barrel
hay field		pine wood

Part II

Even a park in the largest
city has more on every hand
than the largest museum.

– George W. D. Symonds

Part Two—Can You Name It?

The two chapters in Part II will provide a number of games and quizzes, all based on the wonderful world of nature. Use them as *games,* not tests. Take time to enjoy and relish the sound of words.

Children enjoy naming. They enjoy learning the names of things around them, and using these names. Such practice of verbalization has many values. It encourages the child to be articulate. It sharpens the powers of recall and memory. It arouses interest in the object named.

In teaching new words in nature identification, start with the simple, everyday names in nature. As these become familiar, and can be identified, the children will be ready to make more specific identification. A sparrow can become a *fox* sparrow; a pine tree can be recognized as a *white* pine; an aster can be identified as a *New England* aster; a rose can become Peace, or Tropicana.

Learning names often comes before learning to identify that special object. Many games are based on naming, with or without identification. They are very useful for hot weather, or for times when the children are tired or restive. They are even more useful when they are followed up on trips, hikes, or in books, by finding out *more* about each object than its everyday name.

CHAPTER 6

Nature Name Games

These games are interest builders. These games are word builders. Best of all, they're *games*. Play them for fun, and the other values are bound to be included.

Whenever possible, follow up these games. Make a collection of Nature's Travelers. Look for, examine and identify the flowers whose names make such good charades. Collect the leaves of all the trees listed in Tree Bingo. Use the nature material common to your area.

Nature's Travelers

Each person collects as many different kinds of nature's travelers as he can find, and brings them back for identification. Try looking at them through a magnifying glass, to see how they're made. Look for such items as:

Seeds with *wings,* such as box elder, ash, maple.

Parachute seeds, such a dandelions, milkweed, catalpa, buttonball tree, cattails.

Seeds with *hooks,* like burrs, beggar-ticks.

Seeds that *shake* out, like poppies and colombine.

Seeds that *pop* out, like jewelweed, violets.

Food Fun

Many boys and girls have never thought about the food they eat, except whether it's hot or cold, good or bad, or whether there's a second helping. A trip to the nearest grocery store, supermarket, or vegetable garden will be the best way to follow up these questions. It will be a good way to introduce the youngsters to the names of various plants, what they look like, how they grow, what part of the plant is the edible part.

Try to find and study the *whole plant.* What sort of flower does the tomato plant have? Rub its leaves and see how they make the hand yellow. *Smell* the leaves. Plants are like people; they're more interesting the more you know them.

What *roots* do we eat? Add others.

| beet | radish | salsify |
| carrot | turnip | parsnip |

What *leaves*?

| spinach | lettuce | parsley |
| watercress | endive | kale |

What *stems*?

| rhubarb | leek | celery |

What *fruits*?

string beans	wax beans	peppers
egg plant	lima beans	rice
peas	okra	squash
corn	cucumber	watermelon
tomato	pumpkin	cantaloupe

What *sap*?

maple sugar   sugar cane

What seeds make our bread?

wheat   rice   oats
        barley   rye

A Square Meal

Here's a good game to play just before lunch or dinner. It whets the appetite. The block of letters on a sheet of paper or an index card can be prepared ahead of time, or the youngsters can write them down as they are read off.

```
K E R S M S T A
C A R L A B E V
T E B C H E S I
U L G R E A D V
A C O A N M N E
K R O P S O N A
E I S E C A N L
C S P S A S B E
```

Beginning with any letter in the chart and moving one letter at a time in any direction, each person tries to spell out the names of articles of food, drink or seasoning. Use the same letters and squares as often as necessary, and begin a word anywhere in the square. Play for only a few minutes and award some foolish food prize to the winner. Here are forty words which can be spelled from the letters in the square:

lamb	ale	clams	crab	hen
beets	kraut	bread	corn	aspic
damson	cake	grapes	bananas	mead
beans	pork	cream	bran	roe
bacon	pecans	kale	ices	sage
peas	goose	endive	mace	sago
rice	ham	veal	spice	scone
tea	beer	cress	pie	crackers

A score of 40—You're a real chef!
A score of 30—You're a real gourmet!
A score of 20—You're still hungry!

Construction Engineers

Try to find a bird's abandoned nest. Each child chooses some one type of building material that he thinks will be found in it— evergreen twigs, grasses, strips of bark, moss, etc.

They pull the nest apart, *very* carefully, bit by bit, making separate piles of each separate building material.

The first person who can identify an unknown item can claim it.

Follow-up: Try to locate the *sources* of the building material. Where is the nearest evergreen tree? What vine did the bark come from? Where is that special moss found?

Tree Tag Day

A fine game *after* the children have become fairly familiar with tree identification.

Each person gets ten tags, each tag with the name of a tree common to that area. In twenty minutes, each must locate those trees, and pin the correct tag five feet high on the north side of the correct tree. No tree may have more than one tag.

Follow-up: Call in the tags. "Bring in all the oak tree tags." The children dash to find all of these, then the maples, pines, etc. The person with the greatest number of tags wins. Use the names of trees familiar to your area.

Categories

Select some category, such as *Birds.* Each person in turn names a bird that has not been named by anyone else. He must do this before you can count to five. If he misses, he drops out and waits for the next category. The last person left wins.

Variation # 1: Name the birds alphabetically (albatross, bittern, etc.).

Variation # 2: Name a bird whose first letter starts with the last letter of the previous bird. For example, person # 1 says *wren*. Person # 2 tries to think of a bird whose name starts with *n* and comes up with *nightingale*. Person # 3 adds *egret*, and so on. This is a hard way; save it for those who know birds.

Variation # 3: Play Categories with *animals, fish, flowers,* and *trees.*

Combine categories into the familiar, written form. Select several letters and several categories, and make up a chart such

	A	C	T	F
BIRDS		CRANE		
ANIMALS	ANTELOPE			
TREES			TULIP	
FISH				FLUKE

as the accompanying one. Each letter space must be filled in with a name in each category. Then when everyone has finished, compare the names used.

Any name used by only one person counts five points for him. If used by only two people, each gets four points. Any name used by every player doesn't count.

Alphabet
Similar to Categories. Each person, in turn, tries to think of a name in a category (such as Animals, Birds, etc.) starting with *A*. When each has had his turn, # 1 starts with *B*, and so on.

Variation: Play with two teams facing each other. First person starts off with a name beginning with *A*. The one opposite him tries to name another, then back to player # 1, etc. When one player can't think of a name and the opposite person can, the latter's team wins a point, and the next player starts with the next letter.

46

From Where I Sit

A good game to play while resting or looking at an interesting view. Each child takes turns in naming one thing at a time that he can see from where he sits, but which has *not* been named before.

Tree Bingo

Prepare in advance a list of about thirty names of trees and keep this hidden. To start the game, give each person a large sheet of paper and ask him to draw five lines each way from margin to margin, making twenty-five squares. On a signal, each starts writing the names of as many different trees as he can think of, one in each block, until all the squares are filled. Wait until everybody finishes filling the squares, and give a little prize to the first.

Then read the previously prepared list slowly while each player crosses out on his own sheet the names of trees as read. Anybody who gets five crosses in a row vertically, diagonally, or horizontally, calls "Bingo." Keep on reading until the first vertical, first horizontal, and right and left diagonals have been called.

For other occasions, use the names of animals, or birds, or flowers, instead of trees.

Nature Charades

Divide up into two teams. Each team selects some nature name of not more than five letters, such as lion, bear, frog, duck, etc. In turn, each team dramatizes each letter in the name it has selected. The other team tries to identify each letter, and then guess the name.

Variation # 1: Each team selects the name of a flower, and acts out each syllable. Try these:

touch-me-not	carnation
primrose	dandelion
jack-in-the-pulpit	tulip
foxglove	forget-me-not
lady slipper	four o'clock

Variation # 2: Play this game, using *birds, trees,* or other categories of nature.

Variation # 3: Each team selects the name of a bird, and dramatizes it. Try these:

| fly catcher | kite | grosbeak | partridge |
| thrasher | robin | chickadee | woodpecker |

Nature Gossip

Everybody sits in a circle. One person starts by saying the name of some animal. The player next to him must add one fact about that animal, and so on around the circle. Anyone who can't add a fact must pay a forfeit, or do a stunt.

Go Get It

Get the children into two teams, A and B, each with a captain, and number off. The teams stand facing each other, Player A1 facing Player B1, and so on. You stand at the end, an even distance between each team.

To start the game, call out something that you can see, or know is nearby, such as "A leaf with smooth edges—Number 5!" Both players # 5 must dash to get a leaf with smooth edges and bring it back to you. The first to do so scores a point for his team.

Then call out some other item, and another player number, and so on. Items might include:

a white flower	a bit of moss
a pebble that shines	a live insect
a tree twig	a pinecone
a seed	a burr
a nut	a feather

Alive Show-and-Tell

Everyone brings a pet, wild or tame, except cats and dogs. Each owner tells all he can about it—its name, its feeding habits, how to hold it, how to take care of it. Possible pets: chickens, turtles, hamsters, white mice, fish, etc.

Examine the pets carefully. Look for details about eyes, ears, feet, claws, tails, teeth, footprints. What do all these have to do with the way the animal lives, eats and defends itself?

CHAPTER 7

Nature Quizzes

Quizzes can be prepared ahead of time and used with pencil and paper. Or they can be oral quizzes, played informally, or by teams, or in the old spelling-bee manner.

Like nature word games, they should be followed up. Try to find a beaver *lodge* and ant *colony,* watch a *swarm* of bees, a *school* of fish. Go to a farm or children's zoo to see the *ducklings,* not the baby ducks. Build a dog *kennel,* not a doghouse. Visit a zoo and look at the lion and lioness, not just "two lions." Encourage the use of the exact words, for the exact meaning; they are usually the *right* words, much more interesting than vague, general words. Provide an opportunity of *seeing* the objects named, too. It makes them much more real.

Play quizzes. Use them for arguments, discussions and incentives to check up on the facts. Keep them light and interesting. They should not be used like formal tests. If played by more than one player, a quiz has a certain element of competition, but this can be minimized by encouraging self-competition rather than competition against others.

Some quizzes are just for fun. Some stimulate observation, hearing and the other senses. Some are dependent upon the sound of words. In their small way, quizzes are a form of Socratic dialogue, in which questions and answers are used to stimulate thinking.

And *that* is the real purpose; not the accumulation of amusing, useful or interesting facts, but the stimulation of the mind. No quiz will do this alone. The information, to be effective, must be digested, understood, accepted and *used,* so that it becomes a part of each individual.

THE RIGHT WORDS

Many quizzes are good ways to build vocabularies, and to encourage the use of the exact word for the exact meaning. If followed up with discussion, trips, reading, etc., they will stimulate interest—and satisfy it, too.

These quizzes can be turned around and played in many different ways. For example, the leader might say, "If the baby deer is a *fawn,* and its father is a *buck,* what is its mother?" Or "A *cub* and a *vixen* live in a *den.* What is the name of the cub's *father?*" Or "You've heard of *peas* in a pod. What animal group is called a *pod?*"

Animal Groups
Players learn and use the correct words for groups of animals, such as:

sheep (flock)
bees (swarm, colony, hive)
ants (colony)
porpoises (school)
fish (school, run, shoal)

whales (gam, school, herd)
cattle (herd, drove)
seals (pod, herd)
lions (pride)

Animals—Male and Female
lion (lioness)
ram (ewe)
stallion (mare)
gander (goose)
drake (duck)
tiger (tigress)
stag (hind)

bull (cow)
buck (doe)
dog (bitch)
boar (sow)
fox (vixen)
billygoat (nannygoat)

Animal Homes
dogs (kennel)
chickens (coop)
sheep (fold, pen)
pigs (sty)
lions (lair, den)

bees (hive)
beavers (lodge)
pigeons (dovecote)
cows (barn, byre, cow shed)
rabbits (hutch, warren, burrow)

Animal Babies
Players must use the right word for the *young* of such animals as:

lion (cub)
duck (duckling)
dog (puppy)
horse (foal)
cat (kitten)
hog (shoat)
bear (cub)
frog (tadpole)
mare (filly, foal)
elephant (calf)

seal (calf)
deer (fawn)
goose (gosling)
whale (calf)
swan (cygnet)
bird (nestling)
goat (kid)
bull (bullock)
cow (heifer)
fox (cub)

Animal Sounds

What's the word for the *sound* each of these animals makes?

lions (roar)
sheep (bleat)
cows (moo, low)
ducks (quack)
wolves (howl)
crows (caw)
snakes (hiss)
donkeys (bray)
geese (gaggle, gabble)

wild geese (honk)
hens (cackle, cluck)
cocks (crow)
frogs (croak)
doves (coo)
elephants (trumpet)
owls (hoot, screech)
pigs (squeal)

Animal Anatomy

Youngsters are always fascinated by animals, but very often they look at them very superficially. Even more often, they do not know the correct names for the exterior parts. Use such familiar animals as the dog and horse. Study *charts* of these animals, then apply the location to a *real* animal. Practice *using* the right names: a dog's *brisket* or his *withers;* a horse's *fetlock, pastern, hock, elbow.*

Feel the body of a gentle dog. Visit a farm or a riding stable and touch the body of a gentle horse. Seeing, touching and naming all makes the experience much more vivid.

From exterior anatomy, go on further and learn about the *history* of animals. Was a dog always like the modern dog? Was a horse always the size of the modern horse? What part have these animals played in man's history?

Let's Look and See

Other animals are just as interesting. Study, at close range, a pet rabbit, chicken, hamster, goldfish, canary, parrot, parakeet, or cat. Visit a museum and see stuffed specimens of animals and birds. Visit an aviary and see live birds; or aquarium for all sorts of fish and marine life; a zoo for wild animals; a children's zoo, or farm for tame and domestic animals. Whenever possible, *touch* as well as talk. Ask questions. Work up arts and crafts projects like *drawing* animals, making casts of their tracks, modeling animals in clay, etc.

Use the following questions as idea-starters, and go on from there. There's no game any more interesting to boys and girls than any game involving living animals. And learning new, interesting and exact words for them is a large part of the enjoyment.

The Rabbit

Does it wash its face?
With both paws?
Is its upper lip split?
How does it hop and run?
Try to imitate it, using hands and legs.
Try to draw its track marks.
Does it fight with its hind legs?
How does it show when it's angry? Frightened?
Are rabbits all the same color?

The Earthworm

Does it have eyes?
Ears?
Feet?
How does it move?
Does it lay eggs?

The Bird

Examine an ordinary chicken for some of these answers.

How many toes?
Does it have teeth?
Does it have eyelids?
How does it swallow water?
Why does it swallow like that?
Why does a bird preen its feathers?
Find the little "zippers" in a feather.
What kind of beak? How does it eat?
From its wings and tail, can you tell anything about its flight
  pattern?
Why do some kinds have webbed feet?
What use are the long legs of some birds?

A Feather

Borrow a microscope, if possible, or use a strong magnifying
glass. A new world will open up! Look at everyday things—a
hair, skin, cobweb, ant, seed.

A *feather* is wonderful.
That central part is the *shaft*.
Those side branches that look flat are *barbs*.
All the barbs together make up the *vane*.
The tiny hooks on the barbs are *barbules*. They're like zippers.
  They can be separated, and then latched together again.
When a bird preens itself, it runs its break over the barbs so
  they'll hook together again.

Speed Limits

Youngsters are always interested in "how fast can it go?" Use these questions to stimulate interest in birds, insects, animals and fish. Why is speed important? Why can one bird fly faster or farther than another? Talk about migrations. Do animals migrate, too?

Encourage youngsters to look at animals in a zoo, or pictures of animals, and try to guess, by their build, how fast they can run. Do the same for birds.

Look up the speed records for piston aeroplanes, turbo-jets, spacecraft manned and unmanned, bobsleds, iceskating, skiing, swimming, track, rowing, different types of horse races, etc. The latest World Almanac will give the latest figures and winners, as well as past records.

THE RIGHT ANSWERS

These questions are based upon facts, or on hearsay, folklore, etc. They may be used as quizzes, but they are also valuable incentives to look-see, or look-up and find-out.

The best way to use them is to find the right answers by observation if that is possible, or by reading followed by discussion and observation.

Just because somebody *says* something doesn't make it true. A skeptical mind is important in learning. "Bill's Grandpa has a friend who says that a hair from a horse's tail turns into a snake if you put it in a jar of water overnight." The answer is "Let's find out!" Visit a farm, a riding academy, or other place with horses, and ask for a horse hair. Put it in a jar. Inspect it in the morning. Has it turned into a snake? Or was the story just a bit of folklore?

Not everything can be solved so easily. The answers to some questions must be found in books, zoos, or museums. But whenever possible, encourage *observing* and *experimenting* to find the right answer and to disprove the wrong answer.

The following are only a few of the possible, sometimes absurd questions. Use them in discussions, and as reason for taking trips, visiting places, and for making full use of all the senses, plus *common* sense! Then add other statements, and encourage the youngsters to be curious, but skeptical before accepting a statement as true.

Some of the quizzes toward the end are strictly for fun. They call for quick thinking, the use of a sense of humor, and the use of words in various relationships. Actually, they're more *human* nature than just nature, but nature words and terms don't always have to be serious and important. If they're happy-making, they'll lead on to the more important topics.

What Do You Think?

The answers to all of these questions except the last three can be discovered by *looking*—looking outdoors, in a zoo, in a museum or in a book. The last three questions are good for name-learning and word-using.

Q: Why do owls move their whole head when they look to the side? *A:* Their eyes are fixed in their sockets, so they can't roll their eyeballs.

Q: Does a bee gather honey? *A:* No, it gathers nectar and *makes* honey.

Q: How many wings does a dragonfly have? *A:* Four.

Q: Where is a bee's stinger? *A:* In its tail, *not* in its nose or mouth.

Q: Does a beaver swim with its front or hind feet? *A:* The hind feet. The front ones are usually tucked under its chin.

Q: Do ducks take off with or against the wind? *A:* Against.

Q: How does a hawk brake his flight when making a landing? *A:* It fans its tail out to its widest.

Q: How does a toad catch insects? *A:* By shooting out its long, sticky tongue.

Q: What is the only bird that can come down a tree headfirst? *A:* The nuthatch, sometimes called "the upside-down bird."

Q: What sort of feet do gulls have? *A:* Webbed.

Q: How does a parrot perch? *A:* Two toes around the perch, in front, and two in the rear.

Q: Are the pupils of a fox's eyes round like a dog's, or oval like a cat's? *A:* Oval like a cat's.

Q: What member of the nut family is shaped like a comma and sounds like a sneeze? *A:* Cashew.

Q: What nut grows underground? *A:* Peanut.

Q: What is the only flying mammal? *A:* The bat.

Q: What animal is born with a tail and no legs, and ends its life with legs and no tail? *A:* The frog.

Q: Name five birds whose call is the same as their names. *A:* Bobwhite, whippoorwill, bobolink, cuckoo, killdeer. (Add others in your area.)

Q: How many descriptive phrases can be named that are based around the names of animals? Such as:

hungry as a bear	meek as a lamb	catty
dog-tired	sly as a fox	brave as a lion

Q: Name the nine planets:

Mercury	Pluto	Neptune
Mars	Venus	Saturn
Uranus	Jupiter	and EARTH!

54

True or False

A woodpecker can go down a tree headfirst.	F
Penguins can fly.	F
Whales belong to the fish family.	F
A baby kangaroo is only an inch long.	T
Fish sleep with their eyes open.	T
Mice can sing like birds.	T
Gorillas eat only plantlife.	T
Cats cannot see in the dark.	T
Giraffes cannot make a sound.	F
Earthworms lay eggs.	T
The mold on bread is the work of an insect.	F
A bat is blind.	F
Squirrels can come down a tree headfirst.	T
Cinnamon is from the bark of a tree.	T
All ants are wingless.	F
The tulip is a native of Persia.	T
The jack-in-the-pulpit, skunk cabbage, and calla lily belong to the same family.	T
Spiders have six legs.	F
All spiders build webs.	F
Earthworms have neither eyes nor ears.	T
Geraniums are native to South Africa.	T
An onion is a bulb and belongs to the lily family.	T
It is the female mosquito that stings.	T
A dog stalks its prey.	F
A cat runs down its prey.	F
A turtle sheds its shell every five years.	F
A toad causes warts.	F
A toad has teeth.	F
If another animal nips off a tadpole's tail or growing leg, these organs will grow again.	T
Tadpoles bite off their own tails.	F
A fish's eyes have no eyelids, but the eyeball is movable.	T
A bird has no throat muscles, so it fills the beak with water and then holds the head up so the water will flow down.	T
Goldfish should be kept in a bowl in the sun and without any plants in the tank or bowl.	F
All plants growing in the house should be watered twice a day.	F
Birds have hollow bones.	T
Snakes are slimy.	F
The ladybug is a beetle.	T
A sponge is a plant.	F
A snake swallows its young in case of danger.	F
A pig is naturally a very clean animal.	T
Cows shed their horns every year.	F
Sheep chew their cuds like cows.	T
Goats eat tin cans.	F

There are over 200 different breeds of dogs known today.	T
The house mouse uses its tail in climbing.	T
The upper lip of a rabbit is split.	T
The teeth of a rabbit are like those of a cat.	F

Variation # 1: Play as if it were a spelling bee. Players take turns answering, and get "spelled-down" when they miss.

Variation # 2: Make a running game out of it. Players form two teams, the True, and the False. They line up about ten feet apart facing each other, and about twenty to thirty feet from a baseline back of each team.

The leader asks a question. If the answer is True, the True line chases the False line, trying to catch as many prisoners as possible before the False line can reach the safety of its baseline.

If the answer is False, the False line chases the True team back to its baseline. Any prisoners taken are added to the team. When all the questions have been asked, the team with the most players is the winner.

Look-Or-Find-Out Quiz

Each person tries to answer the following questions. Those he can't answer he must find out and report later. If it's possible, he may find the answer by observation; if the wrong season, he may look up the answer.

How many stars in the Big Dipper?	7
How many toes has a bird?	8
How many fins has a fish?	7
How many teeth has a hen?	0
How many legs has a titmouse?	2
How many wings has a grasshopper?	4
How many legs has an insect?	6
How many wings has a butterfly?	4
How many legs has a spider?	8
How many teeth does a cow have on its upper front jaw?	0
How many wings has a housefly?	2
How many parts to a poison ivy leaf?	3
If an apple is cut in half, crossways, how many seed divisions can be found?	5
How many apple seeds are usually found in each cell division?	2
How many lobes on a maple leaf?	5
How many wings has a beetle?	4
How many legs has a butterfly?	6

What Tree Am I?

This quiz can be followed up by collecting the leaves of any

56

of the trees native to the area; by learning to identify the trees; by finding out about the trees—where they grow, how they're used, their silhouettes, their fruits.

Quizzes like this one and others that follow are second cousins to riddles and other word games. Many depend upon a double meaning, a change of spelling, or a quick mental conclusion. They stimulate quick thinking, memory, and verbalization. Best of all, they are laugh-making. Start with these:

A tree that is a personal pronoun	Yew (you)
A tree found in some churches	Elder
A tree used by fortune tellers	Palm
A tree that is well-groomed	Spruce
A tree denoting something important in history	Date
To waste away in grief	Pine
What tree is nearest the sea?	Beech (beach)
A tree that is the ———— of my eye	Apple
A mythical tree mentioned in the Bible	Life
Name the double tree	Pear (pair)
What tree will hold things?	Box
What tree will keep you warm?	Fir (fur)
The Egyptian plague tree	Locust
The tree used in wet weather	Rubber
The tree used in kissing	Tulip
The tree used in bottles	Cork
The fisherman's tree	Basswood
A tree whose name is a body of water	Bay
A tree used to describe pretty girls	Peach
An emblem of grief	Weeping willow
The sweetest tree	Sugar maple
A tree which means to make accurate, true and upright	Plum (plumb)
A tree whose name means footwear	Sandal
A tree that we chew	Gum
A tree associated with a boy who became a general	Cherry
A tree left in the fireplace	Ash
A tree whose blossoms are worn by brides	Orange
A tree whose name means stone	Lime
A tree that reminds us of Dixie	Magnolia
The canine tree	Dogwood
A tree whose name means a colored wood	Redwood
The favorite tree of Ohio	Buckeye
The tree that the silkworm likes	Mulberry
The tree whose leaf is a nation's emblem	Maple

Food for Thought

Find the nut, fruit, or vegetable:

What fruit is a double?   Pear

57

What nut is a large strong box?	Chestnut
What vegetable is a machine to raise water plus a relative?	Pumpkin
What fruit is of a Scotch clan?	McIntosh apple
What vegetable is an Indian's wife plus an exclamation of silence?	Squash (squaw-sh)
What nut ought to go well with hot biscuits?	Butternut
What vegetable is a time measure in music?	Beet (beat)
What nut is a sandy shore?	Beechnut
What vegetable is in the alphabet?	Pea
What vegetable is on the breakfast menu, plus a factory?	Eggplant
What vegetable is a reverse plus small bites?	Turnips
What nut is good for dunking?	Doughnut

Anatomy

What parts of the human body are suggested by the following terms?

Two lids	Eyelids
Two caps	Kneecaps
Two musical instruments	Ear drums
Two established measures of length	Feet
Articles a carpenter cannot do without	Nails
Two tropical trees	Palms
Two spring flowers	Tulips (two lips)
Two playful domestic animals	Calves
Small wild animals	Hares (hairs)
Weapons of warfare	Arms
A number of weather cocks	Vanes (veins)
A tavern stair	Inn step (instep)
Terms used in voting at a meeting	Ayes and nos (eyes and nose)
Two students	Pupils
A large box	Chest
Church building	Temple
The product of the camphor tree	Gum
A piece of English money	Crown
An article used by an artist	Palette (palate)
A means of crossing a river	Bridge
The 12th letter of the alphabet ending in bows	L-bows (elbows)
An instrument used for church music	Organ
A strenuous college game	Football (ball of the foot)
A military command	Shoulder arms
What a physician claims to do	Heal (heel)
Top of a hill	Brow
A carpenter's connections	Joints
Prison interior	Cell
Newspapers need this	Circulation
A shelter from the storm	Roof
Where a river ends	Mouth

Part III

Life is not so much a matter of discovering something new as it is a matter of rediscovering what has always been present.

— W. Ralph Ward, Jr.

Part Three—Make It and Play It

Nature plays Santa every day. No matter where you are, you can find toy and game material better than anything in the toyshop.

It's a good idea to start a collection box. Any big box that can be divided into different sections will do, or any big box that can hold smaller boxes or bags. Plastic see-through boxes and bags are excellent.

In them store nature-finds, such as round and flat pebbles, shells, acorns, pinecones, milkweed pods, driftwood, seedpods, oak galls, almost anything that can be found. Finding and collecting is a large part of the fun. Use the material of your own locale.

These objects, all from Nature's own collection box, the out-of-doors, can be used in many different ways. Some of these ways are described in the next three chapters. The placement of some of these games may seem arbitrary, but often such activities overlap, and would fit just as well in one chapter as another.

Use these as guides showing how simple game activities can be adapted to outdoor play, and to the use of natural materials. Make up or adapt your own. Encourage the youngsters to change the diagrams, modify the rules, and to make up new games of their own.

CHAPTER 8

Find-Its

All of these games and play activities require finding various types of natural objects, then using them. Looking for, finding and collecting nature's gifts for games is a major part of the fun. Emphasize this part. Try to find *just the right* object—the right color, size, shape, texture, weight. Find and discard. Be choosy. Compare, keep, reject, discuss, admire. It's part of the game!

Flower Puzzle

Collect a number of flower plants (common ones, or flower-garden ones) and cut them into their different parts: flowers, buds, stems, leaves. Mix them together.

The youngsters go over the collection, trying to combine the right parts to make the plants. The person with the most plants made of the correct parts wins.

Find My Flower

Collect leaves from flowering plants such as roses, cosmos, daisies, petunias, nasturtiums, zinnias, marigolds. Each player chooses a leaf, and then goes out to find its flower.

This is a good way to learn to recognize wild flower plants as well as garden flower plants. If the plant is on the conservation list, make this an on-the-spot game. Don't pick!

Leaf Snatch

Collect all sorts of leaves from trees common to your locale, and put them in a large flat box, or in a large pile. The boys and girls form two teams, each team facing the box of leaves that is about ten to fifteen feet away. Call out "a *hickory* leaf!" (or other variety). The first player on each team must dash to the box, find a hickory leaf, and return to his team, going to the foot of the line.

Players # 2 then advance to first place. At the signal, they each dash to the box to find whatever variety of leaf you call for. This goes on until each youngster has had his turn.

The first one back in each dash wins a point for his team, BUT check the leaves! Anyone with the wrong variety *loses* a point for his team. You'll find that this game will encourage quick identification.

Nature Alphabet

Divide the players into teams if the group is large. and work together. If only a few play, each can play as an individual.

Give each child a paper or plastic bag, and a sheet of paper containing the letters of the alphabet. The teams go out, and must find some object starting with one of the letters of the alphabet (such as acorn for "A," briar for "B," etc.) within a given time limit. The person or team with the most letters of the alphabet accounted for, wins.

Nature Calendar

Each person selects his birthday month and makes a calendar for it, decorating it with appropriate objects from the fields or woods.

Pick Up Sticks

A good game for quiet play, or while resting on a hike, or on a rainy day. Gathering and making the equipment is part of the fun, and once gathered, it can be used over and over again.

The youngsters pick up enough fallen tree branches to break up into a hundred or so sticks, each about a finger thick and three or four inches long. These are placed in a bag, basket or pile.

They also collect six peach pits, flat pebbles or other small markers that are not round. Each of these should be numbered on one side only, with a different number from one to six.

Players take turns tossing the markers out on the ground as if they were dice. Each adds up the total of the numbers that can be read, and takes that number of twigs for his score. When all the twigs have been won, the person with the greatest number of twigs wins.

Variation: Divide the boys and girls into two teams. The highest team score wins. Keep a running record for a week and give a weekly award, perhaps a stone that has been gilded to look like gold.

Space Ship and Satellite

Up-to-date variation of an old favorite, using two stones, sticks, vegetables or other objects, different in color. One is the Space

Ship, the other the Satellite. Players form a circle. One player starts the Space Ship zooming around in orbit. The player opposite him starts the Satellite at the same time. Will the Space Ship catch up and pass the Satellite in three orbits?

Stake Your Claim

Teams of two or three players. Each takes a piece of string about six feet long, ties the ends together, stretches it out on the ground so as to cover as large an area as possible, and places stones or other objects on the string to hold it in place. The string outlines the "claim."

One player acts as secretary. The others, inside the claim, report to the secretary *every single thing* they can find *in, on* or *above* their claim. If the name for something found isn't known, the player should make up a descriptive name for it.

When the lists are complete, compare them. What team had the richest claim?

Nature's Toys (Girl Scout-style)

Everybody looks for and finds some twig on the ground that looks like an animal or a creature from outer space, and picks up other small twigs for legs, tails, ears or horns.

With a knife or awl, each person makes small holes in the "body" twig, dips a bit of glue on each smaller twig, and puts it into place. Result: some animal or other wildlife ready for a miniature zoo exhibit.

Variation: Encourage them to create creatures never before seen on sea or land! Call it Life on Mars, or such.

Nature Collage

The youngsters collect all sorts of common, interesting, outdoor objects—twigs, leaves, moss, grass, flowers, pebbles, sand, seeds, burrs, nuts, acorns, cones—the more the better. Then each person takes a piece of cardboard and places his objects on it, trying to work out some arrangement that gives him pleasure.

When he's satisfied with his arrangement, he glues each object into place, using an all-purpose glue. When the collage has dried completely, it will make an interesting hanging, framed or unframed.

Variation: The design can be placed in a plaster of paris mold. This is made by slowly adding plaster of paris to water until it begins to bubble. Stir it just enough to make sure the plaster has all dissolved. When it is the consistency of heavy cream, pour it into a foil pie pan and quickly arrange the design. Poke a hook into the top, so that the collage can be hung.

Butterfly Hunt

The boys and girls study the pictures of various butterflies, and paint or crayon lots of them on thin paper.

Then at some later date when the children are busy with other things, collect all the butterflies and stick a pin or tack through each. Attach them all over the area—on tree trunks, branches, flowers—placing them high and low.

Then have a butterfly hunt. Each person brings back all he can find. Mount them on a large piece of cardboard, a bulletin board, or a tree trunk. The prize? A lollipop with wings!

ACORN PERSON

Gold Rush

Another hunt. Players collect all sorts of stones and pebbles, and paint or spray them yellow. Later on, when the group doesn't see you, hide them all around the playing area. Players must find them, bring them back, and weigh them in, to see who made the biggest gold strike.

Acorn People

Everybody looks for and collects acorns (or other nuts) of various sizes and shapes, with or without acorn cups. Then the boys and girls paint or carve faces on the acorns. With a spot of glue, they place the acorn heads in collars or on stands made of acorn cups or other bits of nature. They can use other acorn cups for hats or ears or make animals out of the acorns. Afterwards stage a tabletop acorn sculpture show.

64

Buzzy B's

The boys and girls collect a supply of burrs—the cockleburr type. They add bits of leaves, grass, etc. for wings, legs, antennae. To display, mount with pins on a sheet of cardboard, or on the bulletin board. Then hold a See-a-Bee Show.

Grass Prints

The group collects as many different kinds of grasses as possible—all sizes and shapes. They mount them in a pleasing design on a piece of black or dark construction paper, and cover with clear plastic film. Or show them how to put the grasses between two sheets of waxed paper and press with a warm iron. Then—a Native Grass Exhibit.

Sky Diver

Each person makes a figure out of twigs, acorns or other natural objects. The parachute is a handkerchief-size square of cloth. The corners of the cloth are each tied to the sky diver with a piece of string about a foot long.

Then roll up the parachute and throw it into the air as high as possible. As it comes down, it will open, and the sky diver will float down.

Walnut Shell Mice

Use half of an empty walnut shell, some cardboard, and a marble for each mouse. Put the walnut shell on the cardboard, draw around it, and cut out the cardboard. Then select a marble slightly larger than the shell is deep. (The shell, with the marble inside, should just clear the table or floor.) In the cardboard cut a round hole not quite so large as the marble, but smooth and large enough so that the marble can turn freely. Other nut shells can be used so long as the marble will fit.

For a tail, tie a 5″ bit of string to the outer edge of the card-

WALNUT MOUSE

board. Glue the cardboard to the shell, with marble inside. Cut mouse ears from paper and glue to shell. Draw eyes and glue on several whiskers of bits of wire, or bristles from a whisk broom.

The walnut mouse will roll down an incline and look very natural.

Walnut shells make very real-looking turtles, too. Try other nutshells for animal and bird variations. Paper-shelled pecans, almonds, hazelnuts and hickory nuts are fun to use for a nature-hunt menagerie. What nuts can you find in your area?

Variation: Make peanut figures, milkweed pod angels and butter-flies—all sorts of creatures made of nature's discards. Learn to look at those discards and see possibilities in them.

CHAPTER 9

Make-Its

Some games require specific playing areas as well as equipment, such as markers, spinners, objects to be thrown or pushed, etc. The playing areas can be chalked on the floor, or outlined on the ground, or in some cases marked off on table tops or cardboard sheets. The equipment can be found in the out-of-doors.

These games have the advantage of being easy to prepare, fun to play, and good to use in the home backyard, playground, or playroom. They can be adapted easily to almost any playing conditions, and are very useful for those rainy, hot, or restless days when nothing seems quite right.

Other play equipment depends entirely for its enjoyment upon the *making* and then *using* the results in camp, backyard or playground activities. In other words, they are means towards a special end, and such motivation makes them very valuable. Whether they are strictly games is really not important. They are in the game spirit, and that's what counts.

Kick Stick

An old Indian game.

Each person cuts and decorates his own, so that it will be different from all the others. Sticks should be about 1" thick and 4½"-5" long. (Keep them and use them in many other games.)

Have the players line up at a starting line, sticks at their feet. At a signal, each tries to get to a finish line first by kicking his stick.

Variation # 1: Play it around a *circular* course. Add obstacles.

Variation # 2: Try using sticks that are partially curved, like a boomerang. They'll move erratically and make the game more difficult and interesting.

Rabbit Hunt

On a table top, or cardboard or other flat surface, mark off the path of the trail, making it wide enough to hold the markers.

If the board is about 11″ x 14″, make the path about ¾″ wide. Draw 88 squares in the path, and end up with a 1¼″ circle lair.

Draw 18 rabbits or any other kind of animal (use one as a pattern for the others) and place them along the trail as in the sketch.

Make a spinner out of a board and short nail pushed through a cardboard circle lined off into six segments. Use pebbles for markers.

Paint the board, both trail and rabbits, so that it looks pretty.

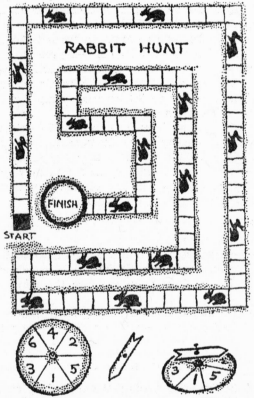

RABBIT HUNT. *Top:* trail. *Bottom:* spinner.

To play: Each child takes turns using the spinner. He can move his marker the number of squares shown on the spinner. If his marker stops on a square with a rabbit, he captures the rabbit. Two markers may rest on the same square with the rabbit, but the first one there is the only one who scores. The player capturing the most rabbits wins.

Variation: Credit ten points for finishing first, five points for finishing second, three points for finishing third, and five points for each rabbit captured.

Snap Board
A type of miniature shuffleboard, good for outdoor play.

Mark off the court on a smooth area outdoors. If indoors, use the bottom of a suit box or a smooth piece of wrapping paper.

Use flat pebbles, sawed-off rounds of small branches, or other fairly flat, natural objects. Find six. There should be three of the same color, or with the same distinguishing mark, such as a crayon dot, and three of a different color.

To play: Players take turns snapping the markers with thumb and forefinger. Three snaps make a round; then scores are added. Set a final score of 100.

Variation: Make a rule that a winner must get a score of exactly 100. If he goes over it, he loses his total score and must start over. Ouch!

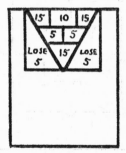

SNAP BOARD

Nine-Men's Morris
Nine-men's morris is a very old game, known also as merels, morelles and mill. Shakespeare mentions it in one of his plays—"and the Nine Men's Morris was filled with mud."

Play the game on an area marked as in the diagram. Make a hole or spot at each intersecting line and the corners of the three concentric squares. Sets of nine men (pebbles, pegs, shells, etc.) are used, one set of one color, one of another.

Two persons play (each having nine men), laying the men down, one at a time in turn on unoccupied spots or holes. The object of each player is to prevent his opponent from placing three men in a row along any of the lines.

As soon as any player has three in a row, he has formed a "mill" and may remove any one of his opponent's men from the board permanently, provided the man is not one of three already in a mill. If, however, there are no other men on the board, he may remove one of three in a row.

After placing all the men on the board, a player may move his pieces forward or backward in any direction that the lines run, but he can only move a man from one space to an adjoining vacant space on the same turn of play.

When a mill has been formed, it may be opened and closed by moving a man one space out (one turn) and one space back (one turn), providing the player's opponent does not block the way. Each time a mill is remade, an opponent's man may be removed.

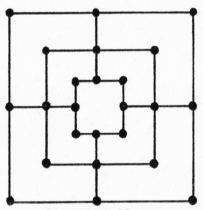

NINE-MEN'S MORRIS

When a player has only three men left on the board, he may move them (one to a turn) to any vacant place on the board and continue to play regardless of lines or positions of other men.

When a player is reduced to two men, he loses the game, as he can no longer form a mill. A player also loses when all his men are blocked in such a manner that he cannot move.

Variation: Reduce the diagram in size, mark it on cardboard, use small markers and play indoors.

70

✓Javelin Throw

Part of the fun of this game is in making the javelins. Each person will need one about five feet long, thick as a thumb at one end, tapering at the other. Willow is a good wood to use.

Decorate by carving the bark, peeling it off in spiral design, or burning a design on it. Each person creates his own design.

Players hold the stick in the middle and throw from shoulder height.

Safety rule: Make sure no one is in the target area.

Friendship Sticks

Short dowels, tree branches, or broom handles can be used. Each child makes at least one friendship stick by sawing or whittling his wood into a stick about a foot long, then decorating it in any way he likes. It may be carved, painted, burned or decorated in any other way. A groove around one end will permit a leather thong or cord to be tied around it, knotted, and used for hanging the stick to the belt, or on a wall.

At a ceremony around a campfire, each person goes before the group and calls out the boy or girl to whom he wishes to give his friendship stick. He then makes the presentation and tells *why* he has chosen that person.

You're It

A simple game, but with an element of suspense that makes it popular with youngsters.

Mark off a large circle on a sheet of paper, and divide it into at least eight segments. Write a direction in each (get suggestions from the group). Then push a pin into the middle of the circle, and put a paper clip over it. Each player takes his turn flicking the paper clip and then following the instruction on the segment to which it points.

Instructions might include such actions as:

> Bring back a leaf shaped like a mitten
> Find a smooth, round, black pebble
> Bring back a stone with a sparkle in it
> Find an acorn in its own cup
> Find a bird feather
> Make a daisy chain and wear it

Variation: Adapt this game to any special nature study—bird identification, weed study, mosses, trees, etc.

Bird Caller

A squeaking sound, such as the sound made by kissing the back of the hand, will draw birds closer. Some say it sounds like a young bird in distress. In any case, birders find a bird caller very useful, and each youngster can make his own quite easily.

To construct, find a piece of hard wood, about 2" long and 1" thick. A piece of old hammer handle will be fine.

A screw eye is needed. Drill a hole in the wood, slightly smaller than the screw eye thread. Turn the screw eye into the hole, take it out, and sprinkle a bit of resin powder into the hole. Then, when the screw eye is twisted back and forth, it makes a fine, squeaky sound. Birds will come nearer to try to find the source of the squeak.

Toy Gardens

Most people, including children, love miniatures. Making a miniature garden is an absorbing activity. It can be a very meaningful experience, since it involves finding and collecting tiny objects from nature, and using them in designing a pretty, tiny garden, planned to scale, and interesting to watch grow.

An aluminum foil or pie tin makes a good container. The bottom should have a layer of small pebbles, then sand, then woods soil full of humus. Into this growing mixture, each person plants his tiny, woods plants or makes a make-believe garden of small twigs, moss, tiny flowers, tiny butterflies, bees, etc. If real plants are used, the soil must be kept moist.

Rubber Band Whistle

Another sound-maker—this time a queer, eerie sound that gets higher and higher the faster it is whirled.

Each person will need a piece of heavy cardboard about six inches long and four inches wide, four rubber bands and a string.

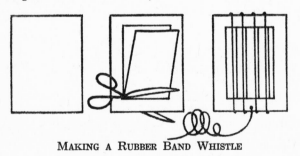

MAKING A RUBBER BAND WHISTLE

Cut out the center of the cardboard, leaving a frame about one inch wide at the top and bottom, and three-quarters of an inch wide at the sides. Make a small hole in one of the narrow ends, and tie a piece of string to it. The string should be about three feet long. Stretch the four rubber bands over the cardboard, across the narrow ends.

To play it, take the free end of the string and whirl the whistle around in a circle. It will soon begin to make its strange sound.

Pickup Stick

For the home, camp or playground cleanup squad. A broom handle or other long stick can be decorated with paint or colored masking tape so that it's gay as well as useful. A nail in one end, and a cord or leather thong around the other end make the stick ready for use. A groove cut around the stick near one end will hold the cord or thong securely, or a hole can be drilled through the cane, and the cord or thong put through it so that the cane can be hung up when not in use. The nail in the other end makes it easy to spear papers, bags, boxes, etc. for the litter bag or trash can.

Safety hint: Keep a cork on that nail when the stick is not in use!

CHAPTER 10

Play-Its

The games in this chapter are fun-making stunts, puzzles and other projects using natural objects when needed. They may be played outdoors or indoors, take up very little room, require a bit of mental effort and are good take-home activities.

Many may be used on rainy or hot days, while resting from physical exertion such as a hike, or while sitting around a campfire, cabin door, or backporch steps. The diagrams, when needed, can be scratched on the ground, chalked on a hard-surface area like a sidewalk or tennis court, or drawn or painted on paper or cardboard. Markers are all around, just waiting for an observant eye to spot them.

Chivas

A skill-and-chance game from Mexico. Each person has a handful of small beans or pebbles, equal number per player. Players line up behind a line eight feet in front of a small hole in the ground, or small bowl. In turn, each youngster tosses all his beans toward the hole. If some go into the hole, he takes these, puts them in the palm of his hand, tosses them into the air and tries to catch them on the back of his hand. Those caught are tossed from the back of the hand into the air and caught in the palm.

The player with the greatest number in the palm, when everyone has had a turn, wins. Try this on teenagers, too. They'll like it; it's great!

Stick Around

A game that even one person can play—against himself. Each person collects a number of small sticks (small twigs are good), pebbles, shells, or other objects. He holds the entire supply in the palm of a hand, tosses them into the air, catches as many as he can on the back of his hand, tosses those in the air and catches as many as possible in the palm of the hand. If he catches an odd number, he keeps one of the sticks and tries again. If he catches an even number, or none, he loses his turn. Set a final score of 11, or 15, and first to get there, wins.

Girls can compete with boys in this simple skill game, and it goes fast! It's a good "what shall I do now?" game.

Kick the Stick

Each person marks off a "course" for himself, using the same number of sticks, stones, clothespins, or other small articles, placed at hopping distance apart. (Finding and placing the articles is a good part of the game.)

When his objects are all in place, each player hops over each one until he gets to the last, kicks it away, hops back, kicks the *first* away, and so on until he has kicked all the items away. First to finish wins.

Variation: Children love to be timed. Use a watch with a second hand, or a stop watch, and time each one. It's double fun to compete against the others *and* improve your own score.

Keeping time is fine with one, two or three players, too. They like the attention of a timekeeper.

Storing Nuts

The youngsters collect nuts, pebbles, acorns, cones, or other small items. They sit in a circle, and take turns. Player # 1 scatters the nuts, then draws his finger between any two, to indicate his choice. Then he picks up one, and from its place, tries to snap it against the other (as in marbles). If he hits it, he keeps both nuts, and draws his fingers between two more. He continues to play until he misses. Then player # 2 picks up all the nuts, scatters them, and tries his luck. Whoever has the most nuts wins.

A good game for two or three players. If more, divide into several games, and let the winners of each play off for top winner.

Jack's Alive

A very good campfire game, or game to play after a cookout in the park or backyard. People played it many, many years ago.

Everyone sits in a circle. Start the game by pushing a dry stick into the fire until the tip glows. Then take it out, blow on the tip to make it glow, and pass it to a player saying "Jack's alive!"

That person blows on it to make the tip glow, passes it to the next player, and says "Jack's alive!" So on around the circle, until finally the stick does *not* glow. The player holding it says "Jack's dead!" and gets a charcoal mark on his forehead. He then must perform some stunt or other forfeit. A very good after-dark game, but be sure to be present when it's played. No burned foreheads!

Four in a Row

A good puzzle for a rest period. Place six leaves or other flat objects in the form of a cross, so that there are four leaves going up and down, and three going crossways.

The object is to move just one leaf so that the cross will form four leaves going up and down, and four going crossways.

The solution is simple—if you think of it! Just take the last leaf on the vertical line and put it *on top of* leaf # 2 of that line!

FOUR IN A ROW

Fox and Geese

An old, old game, taking skill and mental forethought.

Draw the playing area on a piece of cardboard, the ground or other flat surface. Collect 17 "geese"—any small, fairly flat objects, such as pebbles, shells, acorn cups, etc. The "fox" is something larger. Set up the board like the sketch, the fox in the center, the geese almost surrounding him on one-half the playing area.

76

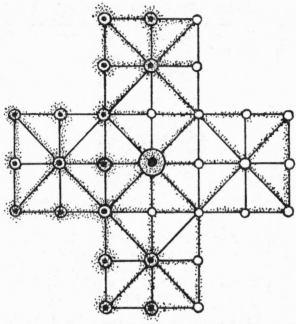

Fox and Geese. Diagram shows layout of playing area at start of game. Shaded circles with center dots are occupied by playing pieces; the central circle by the fox, the rest by the geese.

To play: The fox can move anywhere he pleases. The geese can move only toward the center or sidewise, *never* backward, and cannot pass over two spots at a time. The fox can capture a goose if the goose is on a spot next to it, and there's a vacant spot on the other side.

The object of the game is for the geese to close the fox in so that he cannot move. The game is over if all the geese are taken, or so many are taken that the fox cannot be closed in.

This game improves with practice. Just try it!

Pinpointed

A game of lines, points and markers. Seeds or nuts make good markers.

For group play, draw the accompanying sketch on a floor or hard-surfaced area. For individual play or take-home puzzle, draw it on cards or sheets of paper.

To play: Try to place six markers on intersections so that no two markers are on the same line, in any direction—vertical, horizontal or diagonal. (We made it easy for you by circling the right spots; don't tell!)

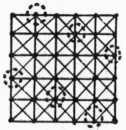

PINPOINTED. Circles show correct placement of markers.

Jungle Paths

Mark off the diagram showing the paths through the jungle, with their openings. Using a stick to mark the way if the diagram is on the ground, or chalk if playing on a hard surface, each person must try to go through all the openings, BUT he cannot crosstrack, or go through any opening more than once.

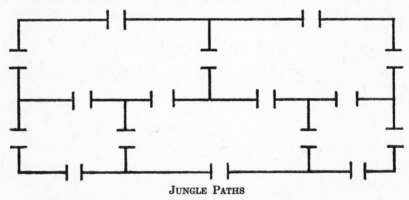

JUNGLE PATHS

Variation: Use as a pencil-and-paper puzzle on a hot day, during a rest period or on a trip.

Nimble Nine

Each person collects nine small objects (acorns, pebbles, shells, etc.) for markers. They take turns at this game, each trying to make the fewest possible moves, and so become the winner.

78

To play: Try to remove eight of the nine objects, leaving the ninth one in the center square. Remove by jumping one over another into any unoccupied adjoining square and taking up the

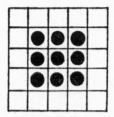

NIMBLE NINE

marker that was jumped over. Jump in any direction, and make any number of jumps with one marker in one move.

Some folks say this game can be won in four moves!

Twig Teaser I

These may not be new to adults, but they are to most children, and they're fun.

The players each collect at least fifteen twigs, as near the same length as possible. They then try to solve the following six problems. Solving four out of the six is good, five is excellent, and all six is SUPER. Solve them one at a time. Place the twigs in the puzzle position, as shown on p. 80, then rearrange into the correct answer.

1. Change the position of four twigs to make three squares, with no twigs left over.
2. Change the position of two twigs to make four squares, with no twigs left over.
3. Take away six twigs and leave ten.
4. Move one twig and make the house face east instead of west.
5. Change the position of three twigs to make the triangle point down instead of up.
6. Here is a way to make four triangles with nine twigs. Can you discover a way to make four triangles with only six twigs? (Hint: this involves the third dimension.)

Twig Teaser II

This puzzle requires twenty-four twigs cut the same length. It's a real humdinger, great for rainy and hot days, or for after a hike, or other relaxed, let's-work-together moments.

The object: To place those twigs into a diagram that will make six squares and twenty triangles. Yes, it *can* be done!

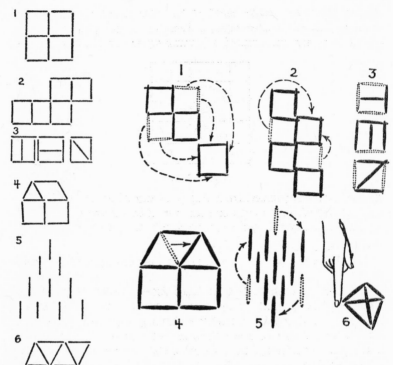

TWIG TEASER I. *Left:* Original placement of twigs. *Right:* Solutions.

SOLUTION TO TWIG TEASER II

Star Trick

Draw an eight-point star on the ground, floor or large piece of paper. Place a pebble, acorn, pinecone or other small object on any point, slide it along to the opposite point, where it must stay; that point cannot be used again as a starting point. For example, if the acorn is moved from H to C, it must stay on C, and C cannot be used as a starting point.

The object is to get a marker on each of the eight points. Keep a record of the time each player takes; shortest time wins. Or let them struggle over the puzzle, because it's not easy, unless you know the answer.

Solution: Always follow each move with a move that comes *back* to the starting point of the one before. For example, if the move was from H to C, the *next* move should be from E to H. The third move would start from B to cover E, etc. Easy when you know how!

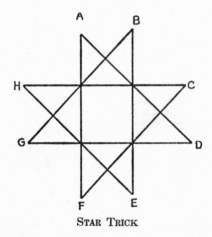

STAR TRICK

X Marks the Spot

Another line game, using eight markers of nuts, seeds, pebbles or such. Mark off the lines, as shown in following sketch, on cardboard, chalk them on a hard-surfaced area, or line them on the ground.

To play: Try to put one of the markers somewhere on each line so that no two markers are diagonal, horizontal or vertical. See sketch for the answer, but don't tell!

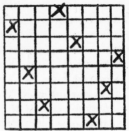

X MARKS THE SPOT. Correct placement of markers is shown.

Lost in the Woods

Another game to be outlined on a cardboard, or chalked on a hard-surfaced area, as shown in the sketch of the game.

The den with the star marks the place where the player is lost in the woods. He must get out by finding a way to the edge, using only even-numbered squares.

3	2	4	2	8	4	4	8	5
2	8	1	7	8	6	7	6	4
6	5	6	4	6	1	2	9	6
6	1	3	5	8	3	2	4	5
4	9	8	4	☆	4	8	7	6
8	2	7	1	9	8	9	2	6
5	2	2	8	5	8	4	7	4
1	4	3	9	2	6	2	5	4
7	6	2	2	6	9	8	6	3

LOST IN THE WOODS. One possible escape route is shown.

Then he must try to find another path out of the woods, using only odd-numbered squares. He may move up or down, left or right, or diagonally.

Daisy Take

Everybody knows the old game of picking petals from a daisy to find out whether "he loves me, he loves me not." Many also have used the daisy petals to foretell the future: "Rich man, poor man, beggarman, thief; Doctor, lawyer, merchant, chief."

There's still another game to play with daisy petals. Two players take turns pulling one or two adjoining petals. The object is to take the last petal, leaving only the stump for the loser.

There's a formula, which if used, makes it certain for a player to win, no matter who starts off first. See if the players can figure it out.

Here's the secret. To win, just use the magic number 3. If the other player takes one petal, you take two, because one and two add to three; when he takes two, you take one. If no daisy is available, draw one like the sketch, only larger, and put a pebble on each petal.

DAISY TAKE

Part IV

> *Indirectly, you are raising children of good will when you keep alive a child's eager curiosity about the world around him. . . . A feeling of reverence, for all forms of life can carry over to respect for all kinds of people.*
>
> *— Edith Neisser*

Part Four—Finders-Keepers

The suggestions following in Chapters 11 and 12 are classified loosely as treasure hunts and scavenger hunts. The differences between these types are minor, and in many cases one type could just as well fall under the other classification.

Basically, those nature hunts that require the laying and following of clues or the finding of natural objects *on the spot* are treated as treasure hunts, which may or may not result in the finding of any actual treasure in the form of some sort of treat.

The scavenger hunt, on the other hand, requires the finding and the *collecting* of various natural objects under specified rules and regulations.

Both types are familiar activities, often used for home, neighborhood, camp or social events. Those included in this book, however, have been chosen because they arouse curiosity and satisfy it; generate the excitement and suspense of the chase, but with no harmful results to plants or animals; encourage the identification of plant and animal life, and a respect for all living things.

Both types are interesting, educational and fun. Both have another feature in common; they must be *planned*.

CHAPTER 11

Treasure Hunts

In planning treasure hunts, two general methods of managing the clues can be used. One method is to give each player a list of instructions and clues. The other method places each instruction and clue along the route, so that when clue # 1 is found, it gives instructions for finding clue # 2, and so on.

Treasure hunts may be played with each player hunting separately, or if the group is larger, in pairs or in teams.

The trail must be laid ahead of time. It can be laid from the starting point, each clue location chosen carefully along the way, and leading by devious ways to the final point where the treasure is hidden.

The favorite, and time-saving way, however, is to start with the treasure location, and work *back* to the starting point in laying the clues.

Clues: The way the clue is prepared helps to set the atmosphere of the treasure hunt. The following are only a few out of many successful ideas:

Treasure maps. Made from torn pieces of paper, edges scorched, clues written in red ink (blood!).

Capsules. Clues written on small strip of paper, then inserted in a large capsule. These are available from any drugstore, and very inexpensive.

Bark. Clues written on birch bark from fallen or dead trees.

Animal cutouts. Clues written on the back of each.

Flower cutouts. Same.

Bird cutouts. Same.

Poems or jingles. Rhymed clues, such as "For the first clue to the Treasure Trove,/ Look under a stone in a small pine grove."

Trail marks and signs. Piles of stones, bunches of grasses, broken twigs, all so arranged as to point the way straight ahead, to the right, to the left, etc.

Shipping tags make good clue markers. They are strong, can be thumbtacked to a tree or post, weighted by a rock, or tied to a branch.

Each clue should require a *decision,* such as "If this is an oak tree, face south and go to the tallest tree you see. If this is a maple tree, take five steps to the fallen log, look west, and go to the first patch of daisies."

The treasure, if the hunt will lead to some special place for refreshment or other special program, should be something that *everyone* will enjoy, such as a watermelon, a bag of candy, cold drinks, or lunch. It's a good idea to wrap it in a dark cloth or put it in a box and tie it up in a tree. It will be less conspicuous there and more difficult to locate.

It is sometimes a good idea to lay the trail in a circular path, so that the youngsters eventually return to the starting point for their treasure. A "home crew" can be stationed there, to prepare the refreshments and to be ready to start any game or stunt program.

The types of treasure hunts that follow are primarily involved in nature activities—the identification, observation and enjoyment of plant and animal life in its natural environment. Some are suitable for, or may be adapted for use in backyard and other neighborhood settings. Nature, after all, is all around us.

Secret Numbers

A two-way treasure hunt. The youngsters must find all the notes placed around the area, whether backyard, camp, playground, street, or other neighborhood spot. They must also come back with the right score. *You,* of course, have already gone over the area and know the answers.

This is a particularly good type of hunt because it promotes careful observation, stimulates curiosity, and is an exciting game, all at the same time.

Number the notes. *Players must find them in order;* no one can open note # 3 until he has found and read # 2. This sort of hunt can be played with even one child. If more, send them out in small groups of twos and threes.

The notes can include such observations and instructions as:

> *Note #1:* Line up at the fence and walk carefully forward, counting your steps, until you see an anthill. Write down the number of steps you took.
> *Note #2* (at the ant's nest): If the ants in this hill are all black, add 100; if they are partly red, add 500. Turn to the right and walk carefully until you see a spider's web.
> *Note #3* (near the web): If all the threads in this web are sticky, add 5. Look around you and walk to the nearest tall tree.

Note #4 (at the tree): If you see one bird's nest in this tree, add 10; if you see three nests, add 30; if you see none, add 100. Walk back to the path and look for a snakeskin along the edge.

Note #5 (near the snakeskin): If this snakeskin is right side out, add 10. If it's wrong side out, subtract 10. Walk down to Mr. So-and-So's field (or yard).

Note #6 (near the edge of field): Look for weed seeds. Add ten for each different kind that can stick to your sweater or socks. Walk down to the road (or sidewalk).

Note #7 (at edge of road or sidewalk): Find a stone that will make a yellow mark on the sidewalk. It is probably limonite, an iron ore. Add 10 if you find it. Come back to the starting place and add up your score. If it is less than 500, look *up* and find the treasure. If it is over 500, look *down* and find it.

Variation # 1: Secret numbers can be made easier or more difficult, to suit the nature information level of the players. Other notes might read like these, and need not have a time limit.

Note #1: This tree is a white pine. The secret number equals the most common number of needles found in each bundle on this tree. The next note will be found at the base of the largest tree you can see to the south of this point.

Note #2: This tree is a sugar maple. If the leaves of this tree are arranged in twos opposite each other on the twig, the secret number is 10. If the leaves are alternate and not opposite, the secret number is 5. The next note will be found under the "skin" of a large stump. Continue south along the trail.

Note #3: Each ring on a stump indicates one year of growth. If this tree was more than fifty years old when cut, the secret number is 20. If the tree was less than fifty years old when cut, the secret number is 10. Continue along the trail and look for the next note in the first drainage pipe under the trail.

Note #4: The secret number is 30. Follow this stream in a downstream direction to the next bridge. The note will be found under a rock on the south end of the bridge.

Some things to keep in mind in conducting a hunt of this kind:

The best game for a group of beginners would be one in which very little actual knowledge would be needed but the success would depend on keen observation.

Use as many kinds of nature materials as possible—stones, trees, work of insects, flowers, bird nests, etc.

This game can be adapted to children or adults by increasing the difficulty of finding clues and making observations.

Emphasize the fact that accuracy, not time, is the chief element in success. Warn players to leave notes undisturbed for groups that follow.

Appoint or have a captain chosen for each group and supply him with pencil and paper for the recording of numbers from each clue.

Give the captain the directions to the first clue and explain the game to the group.

Variation # 2: Omit the use of secret numbers and make the finding of the next clue based on observation. For example, if clue # 3 is located at a cement cornerstone, the following statement might be made:

> *Clue #3:* If this cornerstone is *nature*-made rock, continue down the street and look for the next clue at the base of the gatepost at the park entrance. If this cornerstone is *man*-made rock, go back along the route you have come and look for the note under the first maple tree you come to.

Neighborhood Treasure Hunt

In a city situation, an observation treasure hunt can be worked out based on shade trees, gardens, materials in store window displays, etc. Work out a series of questions that could be answered briefly or with a single word. Directions may be given using street numbers.

The following illustrations may help to show how this game might be worked out:

> *Note #1:* Go to 1218 Fourth Street (a department store). List one object in the window that originated from each of the following: mammal (wool scarf), plant (cotton gloves), insect (silk dress).
>
> *Note #2:* Go to 1311 Fourth Street. The tree in front of the house is dead. Did the injuries near the base of the tree take place before the tree died or after the tree died? _____ How can you tell? _____
>
> *Note #3:* The next station will be at 522 Dory Street. Notice the cedar trees beside the walk. Can you find more than one kind of foliage growing on the same tree? _____

Fifteen to forty questions may be worked out. If the number of players is large, the questions may be mimeographed. For small groups, a few carbon copies would be sufficient. Send the youngsters out in groups of four to eight and emphasize their working together. On the return from the trip, discuss and correct the answers. The last clue should help to locate the reward.

Tree Treasure Hunt

A trail or treasure hunt in which all clues are placed on trees, and each tree must be recognized in order to find its clue.

Players get the first message, such as "Go down the North Road until you come to a tree *much* bigger than any others in sight. Reach as high as you can, and you'll find the next clue." The next clue might say "Go toward the sun until you come to an evergreen tree. Look for the clue on one of the lower branches," and so on.

This sort of hunt can be made easy for inexperienced players, or much harder for players who are good at identification. Fit the distances and the clues to suit the ages and experience of the players.

INFORMAL HUNTS

These are good for change of pace, for surprises, and for that "what'll we do now?" feeling.

Dinosaur Egg Hunt

Paint or crayon small paper or cardboard watermelons, and hide them in the playing area. Keep a count. Players all spread out and try to find as many dinosaur eggs as possible. The player with the most gets to choose his slice of the cold dinosaur egg (a nice, big watermelon!).

Watermelon Hunt

Hide several real watermelons within the camp or other area, with or without clues. Players hunt until all are found. *And* they must be rolled to the eating place!

CHAPTER 12

Scavenger Hunts

Scavenger hunts are somewhat similar to treasure hunts, but with one big difference. The items listed must be brought back by the player, the couple or the team. Such events can be played in several ways:

1. Each player, couple, or team if the group is large, gets a bag, a list of all the required articles, and starts off at the same time. The first to return with everything on the list is the winner.

2. Each player, couple or team gets a slip with one item on it. That object must be found and returned before slip # 2 is given out. In this way, time may vary with the different items, and a point system can be set up. The player, couple or team that comes back *first* with any item wins a point. The one with the greatest number of points when the hunt is over gets a prize, special favor or other award.

3. Items must be checked off a list when found, but not picked and brought back. This type is best for a nature scavenger hunt.

In scavenger hunts, natural materials should be hunted, but be very careful to list only those that are in profusion, and that are permissible to pick, collect, etc. Stress conservation, private property, park regulations, etc.

When played in a picnic area, or where there is litter, add it to the list. The hunt can help in a cleanup job.

Items on a nature scavenger hunt list might include, depending upon the locale, such things as:

pinecone	acorn	shell
dead branch	feather	seedpod
pointed leaf	daisy	round pebble
white pebble	shiny pebble	black pebble
dandelion	shed bark	berry

To these, for foiling litterbugs, add:

piece of wax paper	foil	cellophane
empty bottle	empty tin can	string or wire
paper bag	carton	broken glass

Variation # 1: Scavenger hunts can be limited to some one type of object, such as leaves, nuts, flowers, weeds, vegetables or fruits.

Variation # 2: They can be limited to one special area, such as a beach, stream or meadow.

Variation # 3: They can be very short, or so planned that they become a major event. In such cases, celebrate the return with a special treat of some sort.

ABC Hunt

Following safety and conservation rules, each person or group goes out to collect some object for every letter of the alphabet, or as many of the letters of the alphabet as possible, within a thirty-minute period, or some other time allotment or signal. When time is up, or the signal given, each must return, no matter how many objects he still hasn't found.

When they assemble, each lists his objects alphabetically, such as:

    A: apple (or acorn, ash leaf, etc.)
    B: beetle (or beech leaf, briar, etc.)
    C: catnip (or catalpa leaf, caterpillar, etc.)

Variation: Each person goes off and must find an object beginning with an A. He brings it in to the scorekeeper who checks it off against his name. The player then dashes out after some object starting with B. So on, until someone completes the list or has collected a longer list than the others. Set up a point system, giving extra credit for any item not brought back by any other player.

Individual Nature Hunt

Each person goes off on his own, to find certain objects such as:

    1. Fungus growing from wood

2. Evidence of bad outdoor manners
3. A plant that looks like a fern but isn't
4. An animal home
5. A plant with parallel-veined leaves
6. Food of a raccoon
7. Five different-colored flowers
8. A plant with a square stem
9. A legume
10. A twig with a velvet covering like the antlers of a buck deer.

Note: Each player observes safety and conservation rules.

Shape Hunt

Players learn the *shapes* meant by words like star, crescent, oval (or ellipse), triangle, octagon, hexagon, oblong (or rectangle), spiral (or helix).

Then they set out to try to find some natural object that is somewhat like each of these shapes.

Let-Them-Alone Hunt

The youngsters divide into small groups and each group gets a list of objects common to the area that might be seen on the hunt. The list could include items such as:

A tree that has been struck by lightning	Black ants
A red flower	Red ants
A tree stump more than a foot in diameter	A humming bird
	A small waterfall
Reindeer moss (or other kinds)	Poison ivy
Animal track	Sumac tree
Mushroom	Leaf shaped like a mitten (sassafras)
Maidenhair fern (or other kinds)	
A plant growing in a rock crevice	Flowering dogwood leaf
A bird's nest	Non-flowering dogwood leaf
A squirrel's summer home	White birch
	A hawk

The hunters go together as a group. As soon as a player spots one of the objects on the list, he shouts it out, and his group gets credit. Easy-to-spot objects count one point; rarer objects two or three points.

Part V

I have grown taller from
walking with the trees.

- Karle Wilson

Part Five—Shanks' Mares

The term "hike" is omitted here intentionally, because the main object of a hike is to get somewhere. The main object of the trip and walks suggested in Chapter 13 is to enjoy what is seen, heard, felt, touched and found along the way.

These trips and walks are leisurely. They are quiet, relaxed and restful. They are full of surprises, of new sights, interesting objects to discover, discuss, and find out more about.

Making friends always takes time. It can't be rushed. Making friends with nature is just the same.

Trips and Walks

The suggestions in this chapter are all very simple ones. They all can be modified easily and adapted to any locale. Use them as ideas, to spark your own, and to encourage youngsters to develop their own.

The special interest trips and walks are important in themselves, are fun, and are educational. To get the very best out of them, however, they should be *followed up* by reading, looking at films and slides, looking at objects under a magnifying glass or better yet, a microscope; by discussions; by making collections; by learning names, traits, causes, results.

All these will add to the interest in science. Curiosity is a big first step to stir the scientific mind.

Tree Trailing

Fun to play, even if you don't know a single tree! More fun if you do! If you don't know the names of the trees, just use descriptions. These will require observation and decisions by the youngsters. And you all can pull out a tree book later.

Work out your own directions. They might read like this:

1. Start off by touching the trunk of the biggest tree in sight (perhaps an oak).
2. Go to a tree with loose, rough bark (a shagbark hickory).
3. Not far off, find a tree with a trunk that looks as if it had muscles (ironwood or hornblow).
4. Look for a small tree with some leaves that are mitten-shaped (sassafras).
5. Go to a tree with very smooth, gray bark (beech).
6. Look around and find a tree whose leaves always seem to move (aspen, poplar, sycamore).
7. Walk to the nearest tree with needles (pine, hemlock).
8. Touch the trunk of a tree that has loose, smooth bark like paper (birch).
9. Hurry back to the starting place.
10. Where's that tree book!

Adventure Trails

Get the boys and girls together and go exploring into an outdoor area that's unfamiliar—a park, a beach, a swamp. Take time to explore its sights, sounds, smells; its bird and animal life; its grasses, weeds, trees, flowers. Enjoy and observe. Share what you know about what you find. Admire and examine the items you can't name, and look them up later.

Bring-Them-Back-Alive Trip

A trip to find, watch and collect small living things, such as beetles, worms, ants, insects, caterpillars. Bring them back alive, study them, find out their names; then let them go.

Trail Reading

Select a definite path or trail ahead of time, and if necessary, place certain inconspicuous natural objects where they are in plain sight. For example, a small log across the trail, a picked flowerhead on the edge, a white rock under a tree, a stump, etc.

Don't tell the youngsters about the test. They walk leisurely to the end of the trail, then try to answer ten questions based on what they have or could have seen along the way. Walk back over the trail and verify the answers.

This can be played in a backyard, or along a street, and it's a good way to encourage observation and memory. Children enjoy its challenge.

Rainbow Hunt

Everybody keeps a list of all the different colors he sees on the hunt. Compare them afterwards and see how many different colors were seen.

Treasure Walks

Take the youngsters on a short walk or hike. Each one searches for his own special treasure—something interesting or beautiful which he would like to remember. No touching, no collecting. He stores it in his *mind,* not his pocket. At the end of the walk, everyone shares his treasure by telling about it.

Trail Throwaways

Each person starts on the walk or hike with ten pebbles, nuts, acorns or other small items. As the group moves along, call out the name of some tree or flower. The person who dashes back first with a leaf of that tree, or the flower named, may throw away three of his markers; the second to return may throw away two markers, and the third may discard one marker. Keep on playing until all the markers are gone.

Hares and Hounds

The old paper trailing, but without litter. One group, the Hares, gets a headstart of ten minutes—long enough to get out of sight. It leaves a trail by dropping some special leaf.

Variation # 1: The Hares carry a supply of small twigs and stick them, pinlike, through leaves that are in plain sight along the way.

Variation # 2: The Hares pin small paper butterflies on objects along the way. The Hounds must collect them all, and keep count.

Variation # 3: The Hares leave small rabbit cutouts, made beforehand, along the trail. The Hounds must collect and bring them all back.

Warning: Make removal of any clues part of the game. No litterbugs, even in play!

Quests

Prepare a listing of possible discoveries to be looked for on a trip or hike. If you don't know their *names,* ask for samples that *look* different. For example, "Two ferns that look different," rather than "Two kinds of ferns." You can always look up the names later! Your list might include things like:

> two kinds of spider webs
> squirrel's summer nest
> bird nest not more than six feet from the ground
> two kinds of hitchhiking seeds (burrs, etc.)
> winged seed
> two kinds of mosses
> red-winged blackbird (or other bird)
> two kinds of ferns
> red flower
> beetle
> animal tracks
> three kinds of insects

Variation # 1: Rate the objects in terms of difficulty of finding. For example, spider webs might count five points because they're harder to find, whereas a winged seed might count only one point.

Variation # 2: If played in the backyard or if the trip is around the block, on the beach or in the park, make out a list of objects that can be found by looking hard. Include garden flowers, fruits, ants, bees, weeds, pebbles, shells, birds, etc. They might escape notice, but they are there for seeing eyes to find.

Tree Claims

A good game to break up the monotony of a walk or hike. Once in a while (not too often), call out the name of a tree that is plentiful in that area, perhaps "Pine!" All the hikers dash to claim a pine, one player per tree. Each player gets a pebble or bean every time he "claims" a tree. He keeps his awards until the end of the walk. The player with the greatest number gets a special treat.

Nature's Zoo

Each person gets a set time—fifteen minutes or half-hour, depending upon the locale—to find some natural object that looks like something else, or that can be *made* to look like something else by adding a berry for an eye, a feather or other natural objects.

Driftwood, roots, bark, cones, stones, seedpods, shells, vines, tree branches and twigs are possible sources. Everybody finds his own and prepares it for an all-group exhibition.

Nature's Discards

Everybody looks for and collects discarded remnants such as:

castoff snakeskin	bark strips	seeds
fallen leaves	seedpods	velvet from deer antlers
lost feather	burrs	nuts

Combine them at end of walk, and try to identify each. Then use them in make-something program.

Oddities

Go on a walk or ramble. Everybody looks for something that is unusual or odd—such as a humpbacked tree, a twin-trunk tree, a nut gnawed by a squirrel, a strange-looking knot on a tree trunk, a stone that looks like an animal or a face, a queerly marked leaf or bark, etc. This game requires observation *and* imagination—two fine qualities.

Parasites

Players on the walk or trip try to observe as many different kinds of parasites as possible. Look for such parasites as:

mosses	lichens	mushrooms
mistletoe	Indian pipes	beechdrops

If your area has few or no real plant parasites, look for hitch-hikers, such as many of the seeds and burrs that are carried away by outside forces such as wind, animals, birds and man.

Pitfalls

Players on the trip or walk try to spot all the natural pitfalls or booby traps possible, such as:

spider webs	rabbit holes	prairie dog holes
anthills	wasp nests	mole runs

Color Walks

One person looks for as many objects as possible that are red. Another chooses blue, another yellow, etc.

Variation: Everybody goes on a *yellow* walk today, a *blue* walk tomorrow, a *red* walk another day. It's amazing how color-conscious the players will become. Keep lists. What are nature's favorite colors? Do the favorites change with the seasons?

Progressive Hike

For arousing new interest in familiar areas, and giving everybody a chance to be the leader. Prepare numbered notes for quests using one or more of the senses. The first person to find the object of the first quest shows it to the group and becomes the leader up to the next stopping place. Add some little stunts or special requirements, just for variation and exercise. Some sample notes follow:

> *Note #1:* Find five leaf shapes. First person to do so must show them to the entire group, and they must do as he does. He must take fifteen giant steps and ten lady steps in the direction his shadow points, then read Note #2.
>
> *Note #2:* Close eyes and listen. First person to identify four natural sounds may take group on a four-legged walk to nearest big rock, tree or other object and read Note #3.
>
> *Note #3:* Go to the nearest evergreen (or other) tree, and look for signs of insects within ten feet. If six signs can be found, go twenty steps; then walk like a crab (sideways) for twenty feet. If less than six signs can be found, return to the rock and tell a rigmarole story about how the rock came to be there.

Tag Day

Collect or make some cardboard tags, each with a string attached so that the tag can be tied on something. Give each person the number of tags he'll need to follow the instructions. If the group is as large as six or more, better divide it into teams of two, three, or four, so you won't need so many tags! This game can be used to make nature trails for others to follow if you can write additional information on the tags.

Tell each youngster to put a tag on:

1. Two kinds of soil-building materials.
2. A place where some animal is making use of the trees.
3. A place where water is eroding and washing away the soil.
4. A spot where man has interfered with Nature's plans.
5. A spot where Nature has healed her own wounds.
6. A good spot for a bird or small animal to gain protection from its enemies.

Accident Cases

Everybody looks for all examples of accidents or untimely death along the way, such as a:

rock split by a tree root	shell with a hole bored in it
tree blown down by the wind	animal hit by an automobile
tree cut down by man	feather
tree struck by lightning	nut gnawed by a squirrel
tree or land area burned by fire	broken spider web
empty shell	fish thrown up by the tide
leaf partly eaten by an insect	anthill that has been stepped on
fern or plant that has been stepped on by somebody	dead flower

Locomotive Walk

Everybody looks for examples of how wild things *move,* using such means as:

wings	fins	spines	tails
scales	legs	muscles	claws

See how many *ways* of moving can be found:

climbing	flying	crawling
jumping	running	rolling
sliding	swimming	burrowing

Other Special Interest Walks

The possibilities of them are almost endless, and every one of them will make any walk or hike more interesting. You don't have to be a naturalist to enjoy any of these. Just use your eyes!

1. *Discards:* Cast skins of insects or snakes, a fallen leaf, a lost feather.
2. *Transportation:* What is carried by such things as wind, fur of animals, people, birds, insects?
3. *Movements:* Clouds; things blown by wind, such as a poppy cup; animals.
4. *Planters of seeds:* Squirrels, birds, insects, mice.
5. *Tracks, signs or traces:* Animal tracks, leaf prints, dung of animals or birds, nibblings as sign of an animal's having been there for a meal.
6. *Patterns or designs:* Circle radiations (feather), star, dot, triangle or wave.
7. *Signs of the times:* What do you see that is evidence that this is *this* season and no other? Specially good when each season is at its peak.
8. *Homes, homemaking and homemakers:* Spiders, birds, moles, gophers, mice, chipmunks, woodchucks, bees, wasps.
9. *Skins or outer surfaces:* Rock surfaces, bark of trees, feathers, fur, scales, frog and salamander skins, leaf surfaces.
10. *Curiosities:* A plant that has pushed up through a dead leaf carrying the leaf with it; other unusual finds.
11. *Freaks and oddities:* A four-leaf clover or sorrel, a two-tailed lizard, an albino animal or bird.
12. *Miniatures:* Tiny, lovely things, or just queer or interesting, such as the fruiting bodies on moss that look like fairy golf clubs; mosslike plants that are studded with tiny umbrellas or jewel cups; seeds with parachutes or propellers; tiny flowers that you never noticed before, etc.
13. *Remnants of yesteryear:* Birds' nests from last year, leaves, ghosts of flowers, fallen seeds, dried grasses.
14. *Squatters:* Who sits on what? (Parasites, mosses and lichens on rocks, etc.)
15. *Inchers:* Hunt for treasures less than one inch tall.
16. *Cycles:* Plant—bud, flower, fruit, seed, seedling. Frog—eggs, pollywog, frog.
17. *Visitors:* Welcome or unwelcome, helpful or harmful, or neither.
18. *Hitchhikers:* Who gets a free ride? Burrs on socks, ants in lunch, fleas on dog.
19. *Climbers:* How do they climb, plant and animal?
20. *Woodland babies:* Young plants and animals.

Part VI

If I were to name the three most precious resources of life, I should say books, friends and nature; and the greatest of these, at least the most constant and always at hand, is nature.

— John Burroughs

Part Six—How Can You Tell?

All down through the ages, from the earliest days, man has wondered about the stars, tried to foretell the weather, worked out ways of telling time, and used various methods of marking where he has been, so that he and others could return.

Learning how to recognize the signs of rain and storm, evaluating the force of wind and storm, watching nature's calendar of the seasons, identifying the stars in the heavens as they change with the seasons—all these are interesting secrets ready to be solved.

Combining the old ways with man's inventions makes it even more interesting to discover "how can you tell?"

The ideas in this section will focus around weather and the sky. The activities in them cannot be hurried. Observation comes first, then interest, then experiments. Fit them into everyday life by talking about them, wondering about them, guessing, looking up information, experimenting and *using* what is found out.

In these three topics are the seeds of lifelong interest, and the beginnings of lifelong hobbies. Plant those seeds well. Provide the right climate of interest and enthusiasm—and watch them grow!

CHAPTER 14

The Weather

What *is* weather? Is it the same as climate? Discuss these two words with the youngsters and let them try to figure out the difference.

Weather can vary and change very rapidly, even in less than an hour. *Climate* is a sort of average of the weather over a year, in broad terms, like "tropical," "temperate," "arctic."

Look at a world map or globe. Find the Equator, Tropic of Cancer, Tropic of Capricorn, Arctic Circle, Antarctic Circle. What is the general climate of these areas of Earth?

Weather is a combination of many factors: the temperature of the air, its humidity, the amount of rain or snow, the direction and speed of the wind, the type of clouds, and the air pressure. All of these can be measured. All of these are used in weather forecasting.

To forecast weather, five steps can be taken:

1. Observation
2. Collection of other observations
3. Plotting all this information on a map
4. Studying all the information on the map
5. Making a forecast

The study of weather is called meteorology. The weatherman's real name is meteorologist.

Running their own weather bureau is a fascinating game activity for youngsters. It can be played anywhere—in the backyard, on the playground, at the beach, or at camp.

All the projects that follow are simple, easy to do, and require almost nothing special in the way of equipment and supplies. Many of them may be familiar to you, but new to boys and girls. All of them will help youngsters develop more interest in one of the three major elements—the air, without which man could not exist. No wonder everybody talks about the weather!

WIND

What *is* wind? Why is the movement of air so important?

Watch a weather vane, and find out where the wind is *from*. That's the way to read wind directions—the direction it's blowing from, not where it is going. Encourage the youngsters to report on the wind. "The wind is from the south today," "There's a northwest wind today," etc.

Weather Vanes

They tell what direction the wind is from. Look at the different kinds used on houses and barns. Make a simple hand model.

Cut a piece of paper into the shape of a feather and stick it into the end of a soda straw. Use a straight pin, and stick the straw very carefully into the rubber eraser of a pencil. Don't mash the straw. It should be able to move easily. Hold the pencil up in the air. The *open* end of the straw will show the direction the wind is from.

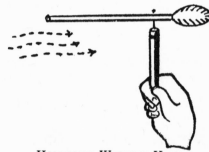

HOMEMADE WEATHER VANE

Anemometer

How fast is the wind blowing? The youngsters can make an anemometer on somewhat the same principle as a pinwheel.

All that's needed is a paper plate and four paper cups with handles. Staple the handles to the plate. The cups should all face the same way. Set the plate on a pin stuck in the end of a stick, so that the plate can move freely.

Does the the anemometer move at all? Very slowly? Fast? Very fast?

Watch the windsock at an air port. What does it show? Is it dangling loose? Does it rise and fall? Is it all puffed out as far as it can be? Does it tell anything about the strength of the wind? How can you *measure* this force?

How Fast Is the Wind Blowing?

There's a *scale* to use. It's called the Beaufort scale, and it'll help the youngsters to learn how to gauge the wind's force. At your own weather station, keep a daily record.

What the wind does	Miles per hour	Name of wind
smoke goes straight up	less than 1	calm
smoke bends slightly	1-3	light air
leaves rustle, weather vane moves	4-7	light breeze
leaves and twigs in constant motion	8-12	gentle breeze
raises dust and paper;	13-18	moderate breeze
moves small branches		
small trees sway	19-24	fresh breeze
large branches in motion	25-31	strong breeze
whole trees sway, walking difficult	32-38	moderate gale
breaks twigs off trees	39-46	fresh gale
damages chimney and roof	47-54	strong gale
trees uprooted	55-63	whole gale
widespread damage	64-75	storm
most destructive of all winds	over 75	hurricane

Weather Flags

Everyone should know these warnings, especially those who live near large bodies of water. The U.S. Weather Bureau adopted them as standards back in 1958.

The youngsters can make a set, learn their meanings, and set them flying at proper times. Visit a local Coast Guard station

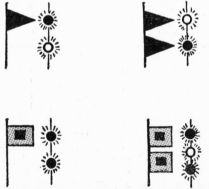

U.S. WEATHER BUREAU STORM SIGNALS. *Top left:* Small craft warning (red pennant by day, red light over white light by night). *Top right:* Gale warning (two red pennants by day, white light over red light by night). *Bottom left:* Whole gale warning (red flag with black center square by day, two red lights by night). *Bottom right:* Hurricane warning (two red flags with black center squares by day, white light between two red lights by night).

if there's one nearby, or when you're visiting a lake or ocean region, and see the real things. During daylight:

Fair Weather: A white square.

Showers: A square, top half white, bottom half blue.

Rain: A blue square.

Small Craft Warning: A red triangle. Wind to 38 miles per hour and/or dangerous sea conditions.

Gale: Two red triangles, one below the other. Winds 39-54 mph.

Whole Gale: Red square, with black square in the center. Winds 55-73 mph.

Hurricane: Two red squares, one below the other, each with a black square in the center. Winds 74 mph or more.

At night, flags can't be seen, so the Coast Guard uses *lights:*

Small Craft Warning: A red light above a white light.

Gale: White light over a red light.

Whole Gale: Two red lights, one above the other.

Hurricane: White light between two red lights.

Newspaper Weather Maps

Study the weather maps in the newspapers. Learn the symbols they use to indicate kinds of weather. It's like knowing a special code!

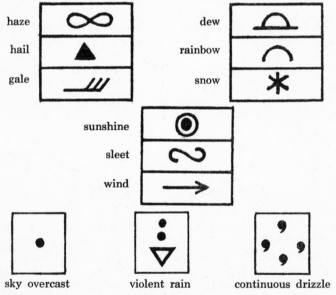

haze	dew
hail	rainbow
gale	snow

sunshine

sleet

wind

sky overcast   violent rain   continuous drizzle

Barometer

Barometers *look* so hard to read, and yet they're really fairly simple. They measure air *pressure*. Each youngster can find out for himself very easily.

HOMEMADE BAROMETER

The National Audubon Society suggests a simple barometer easy to make and to observe. Fill a clear glass bottle about 1/5 full of water. Run a piece of ¼"-diameter glass tubing through the cork, making sure the cork fits snugly. The glass tube must reach down into the water.

Mark the water level with a thin line of paint, or tie a string around the bottle. Then it's ready for use. Watch it from day to day.

When the weather is fair, the air pressure pushes down on the only opening to the bottle, the top of the glass tube, and makes the water level *rise*. As long as the water level stays high or rises, the weather will be good. A bit of food coloring in the water makes it easier to watch.

If the weather is changing, the air pressure gets lighter, and the level of the water will *fall*. Rain is probably on its way.

Rain Gauge

Measure the rain. Make a rain gauge and keep a record. Get a can about eight inches wide; a tall, narrow bottle (olives come in them); a ruler; a bit of paint and a fine brush. Pour water into the can until it measures an inch. Then funnel it into the olive bottle, and write "one inch." Empty it. Then put water into the can until it measures one-half inch, and pour into the bottle, marking this line "one-half inch." Repeat, this time putting in one-quarter inch of water, and mark its level on the bottle.

Then set the can in an open place and brace it so that it won't blow over. After the rain, funnel its contents into the olive bottle, and find out *exactly* how much rain fell. Keep a record, and find out which day has the most rain.

Thermometer (Fahrenheit, after its inventor)

Many youngsters don't know how to use a thermometer, or what the figures mean in terms of heat and cold.

Show each child how to find 32°, the freezing point. Everything below that is below freezing. Does the thermometer show zero? That's c-o-l-d! When the weatherman says it's ten below, what does he mean?

How many degrees does it take to make most people feel comfortable? Where does Dad set the thermostat for the furnace? (Usually it's around 72°.)

When does water begin to boil, under ordinary conditions? (Usually it's around 212°.) Take its temperature and see. Show the youngsters your oven thermometer, and talk about how you use it.

What's the normal body temperature, using an oral thermometer? It's 98.6°, and when it goes higher or lower, it's time to call a doctor.

Clouds

Clouds are weather indicators. They change size and shape, and these different sizes and shapes all have *names*. Young weathermen should learn how to say these names and to identify the kinds of clouds. A few of the most often used names are:

> *Cumulus:* The big, billowy clouds with flat bases. They are often seen on fair days, and when it's windy on such days they break up into smaller clouds and race across the sky.
>
> *Cirrus:* High clouds that look as though they were tufted. They usually indicate a change in the weather, probably a storm or wind on the way.
>
> *Cirrostratus:* These look like cobwebs. When the sky is full of them, rain or snow is usually due in 24 to 36 hours.
>
> *Stratocumulus:* These are big rolls of dark clouds, low in the sky, and they usually mean that a shower is on the way.
>
> *Cumulus-nimbus:* These are big, black "thunderheads." They indicate that a thunderstorm may be on the way.

Sunny- and Rainy-Day Bags

Make two bags of cloth or oilcloth, one for sunny days, the other rainy or cloudy days. One could be yellow, the other blue. Or paint a sun on one, and raindrops on the other. Each sunny day, drop a bean or pebble into the sunny-day bag. Each rainy or cloudy day, a bean or pebble into the rainy-day bag. On the last day of any given period of time, such as a month, vacation, or season, hold a guessing contest to see how many beans or pebbles in each. Best guess for each gets the bag—and a special treat.

St. Swithin's Day Weather Chart

St. Swithin's Day is July 15. If it rains on that day, legend prophesies that there'll be forty days of rain. If the prophecy comes true, the period between July 15 and August 25 will be very wet.

Use a calendar for July and August to test the legend. Check each day twice, morning and afternoon, starting with July 15. Draw a sunny sun if half the day is clear, raindrops if it's raining.

On August 25, count up the sunny and the rainy days. Was the legend right? Almost right? Not at all right?

CHAPTER 15

The Sky

From earliest times, man has watched the sun, the moon, the stars and the planets in our solar system. He has used them to tell time, to mark the seasons, to decide upon planting and harvesting. He has used them in his songs and legends. The very names used today have come down through the ages, when man looked up into the night sky and peopled it with figures of animals and gods outlined in the constellations.

Trying to identify these sky forms and learning their names is possible anywhere—in the backyard, in an open place in the park, or best of all, lying on one's back in a broad meadow on a summer night. Combining this with the tall tales and legends about the constellations, the individual stars and the planets, provides an experience that the boys and girls will never forget.

The Solar System

The nine planets, our Earth one of them, various satellites of the planets, comets, asteroids and meteoroids, make up the solar system. All of them, except the satellites, are held in orbit by the attraction of the sun, which is our nearest star, and around which they revolve. Youngsters can find all sorts of interesting material in the local library on the planets, the stars, comets, eclipses, outer space, and space travel. Just get them interested, and off they'll go.

Sundials

How does a sundial work? The youngsters can experiment and find out.

Stand a pencil in a box of smooth, moist sand. Use a flashlight as the "sun." Make its beam "rise" from below one side of the box to climb up to "midday" and then slowly "set" below the other side of the box. With a pointed stick mark some of the major changes in the pencil's shadow.

Did You Know? ? ?

A quiz, mostly to arouse interest and to show the vastness

of our solar system. It *might* answer some of the questions that the youngsters throw at you!

Q: With good eyes, how many stars can be seen in the night sky? *A:* Around 3,000.

Q: How many stars are there in our universe? *A:* Around 40,000 million. (Try writing that in numbers!)

Q: How long would it take to count that many? *A:* If you counted 100 a minute, and kept counting day and night, it would take nearly 800 years.

Q: How fast does light travel? *A:* 186,000 miles a *second.* Just try to figure out a *year!*

Q: How are star distances measured? *A:* By light years, i.e., the distance light travels in a year.

Observation Projects

Keep a list of what times sunrise and sunset take place. Do they vary? Does the sun always rise in the exact same place, or set in the exact same place? WARNING: *Never* look directly at the sun, not even with dark glasses.

Look for the moon, too. Keep a record. Where does it rise? When? Where does it set? When? What direction are the tips of the moon? Can the moon be seen during the daytime? When?

How long does twilight last? Does the time vary? Keep a record to prove it. If your area doesn't have twilight, see if the youngsters can figure out why not.

Does the Big Dipper (Ursa Major) seem to stay exactly in the same place in the sky?

What direction do the stars seem to move?

The planets? Keep a record and find out.

Planets

Youngsters can learn to identify the planets by location in the sky, brightness and color. Usually planets don't twinkle the way a star does. (That's because they're closer to Earth.)

Try plotting the planet seen. Locate it on a map of the sky, and then check that location every night for several weeks. What direction will it be moving?

Try to locate the area of sky in which the planets are located. It's called the Zodiac.

Look for the hardest to find—Mercury. It's usually visible only at sunrise or sunet, because it's the closest to the Sun. Mercury is the smallest planet. It comes between the Sun and the Earth about once every four months.

Venus is the planet most like our Earth. Look for it just after sunset, in the west or southwest. It is so bright that it's called the Evening Star. Or get up very early; it'll be the Morning Star.

Mars is about half as big as the Earth. It has a reddish color. Look for it directly opposite the position of the sun.

Jupiter is the largest of all the planets, eleven times as big as Earth. It is far away from Earth, but it looks very bright because it is so large.

Saturn is nine times as big as Earth. It's the planet with the rings around its equator.

Uranus and Neptune are so far away from Earth that they can be seen only through a telescope. They are both four times larger than Earth.

Pluto, the ninth, counting Earth, is so far away that it has to be found in photographs of the heavens. It was discovered only fairly recently (in 1930).

Inquire around and see if you can find any amateur astronomer with a telescope. Try to arrange a visit with the youngsters. The night sky through a telescope, seen for the first time, is a tremendous experience for any child.

The table "Facts About the Planets" converts measurements of time and weight on Earth into their equivalents on other planets. Skip this table if you know what it contains, or if you're not interested. Young astronauts will be interested, however.

FACTS ABOUT THE PLANETS

Planet	Distance from Sun (in millions of miles)	Its Year (in Earth time)	Its Day (in Earth time)	What You Would Weigh There (per 100 lbs. on Earth)
Mercury	36	88 days	88 days	38 lbs.
Venus	67	225 days	30 days*	88 lbs.
Earth	93	365.25 days	24 hrs.	100 lbs.
Mars	142	687 days	24 hrs. 37 m.	39 lbs.
Jupiter	483	11.9 yrs.	9 hrs. 50 m.	265 lbs.
Saturn	886	29.5 yrs.	10 hrs. 2 m.	117 lbs.
Uranus	1783	84 yrs.	10 hrs. 50 m.	105 lbs.
Neptune	2791	164.75 yrs.	15 hrs. 50 m.	123 lbs.
Pluto	3671	248.5 yrs.	unknown	16 lbs.*
The sun	—	—	24.75 days	279 lbs.
The moon	—	—	27.33 days	16 lbs.

* Estimated.

If it is at all possible, take the youngsters to visit a planetarium. The most important thing in a planetarium is a giant instrument, set in a bowl-shaped room, and so constructed that it can show how the skies look anywhere on Earth, at any time. The sun, moon, stars and planets can be moved around to show what they are like and how they act. The planetarium machinery can show an eclipse of moon or sun, Northern Lights, and other fascinating phenomena.

Is there a planetarium near you? Here are the ten largest. If these are too far away, inquire about some of the smaller ones in schools, colleges and museums. Over a hundred of these are scattered around the United States, and you very well may be able to find one near enough to visit.

PLANETARIUMS

New York, N.Y. American Museum of Natural History-Hayden Planetarium, 81st St. at Central Park W.

Chapel Hill, N.C. Morehead Planetarium, University of North Carolina.

Chicago, Ill. Adler Planetarium, 900 E. Achsah Bond Dr.

Colorado Springs, Colo. U.S. Air Force Academy Planetarium.

Boston, Mass. Hayden Planetarium, Science Park, Museum of Science.

Los Angeles, Calif. Griffith Observatory and Planetarium, Griffith Park.

San Francisco, Calif. Morrison Planetarium, California Academy of Sciences, Golden Gate Park.

Flint, Mich. Longway Planetarium, Flint Junior College and Community Science Center.

Philadelphia, Pa. Fels Planetarium, Franklin Institute, 20th St. at Benjamin Franklin Parkway.

Pittsburgh, Pa. Buhl Planetarium and Institute of Popular Science, Federal and W. Ohio Sts.

Star Projects

Youngsters study the shapes of the best-known constellations. Then, on a piece of black paper, they pinprick these shapes. When the paper is held up to the light, the shape shows clearly.

Or they can mount the pinpricked paper with masking tape to the bottom of an oatmeal or other cylindrical box, after cutting out the bottom. Light a flashlight inside, and darken the room. The shape of the constellation can be thrown on the wall or ceiling. Hold a sky show.

Star Maps

Another good way to show and to remember the outlines of

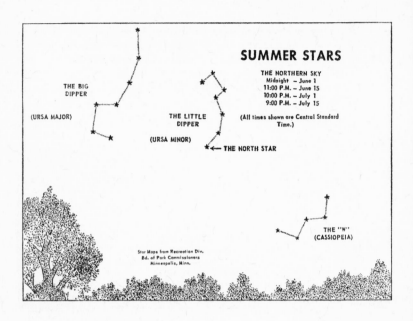

SUMMER STARS

THE NORTHERN SKY
Midnight — June 1
11:00 P.M. — June 15
10:00 P.M. — July 1
9:00 P.M. — July 15

(All times shown are Central Standard
Time.)

THE BIG
DIPPER

(URSA MAJOR)

THE LITTLE
DIPPER

(URSA MINOR)

← THE NORTH STAR

THE "W"
(CASSIOPEIA)

Star Maps from Recreation Div.
Bd. of Park Commissioners
Minneapolis, Minn.

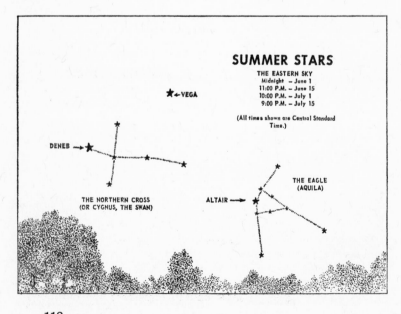

SUMMER STARS

THE EASTERN SKY
Midnight — June 1
11:00 P.M. — June 15
10:00 P.M. — July 1
9:00 P.M. — July 15

(All times shown are Central Standard
Time.)

★←VEGA

DENEB →

THE NORTHERN CROSS
(OR CYGNUS, THE SWAN)

ALTAIR →

THE EAGLE
(AQUILA)

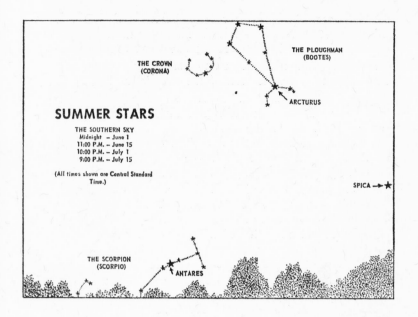

THE CROWN
(CORONA)

THE PLOUGHMAN
(BOOTES)

ARCTURUS

SUMMER STARS

THE SOUTHERN SKY
Midnight — June 1
11:00 P.M. — June 15
10:00 P.M. — July 1
9:00 P.M. — July 15

(All times shown are Central Standard
Time.)

SPICA →

THE SCORPION
(SCORPIO)

ANTARES

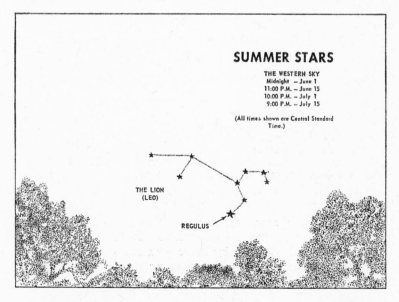

SUMMER STARS

THE WESTERN SKY
Midnight — June 1
11:00 P.M. — June 15
10:00 P.M. — July 1
9:00 P.M. — July 15

(All times shown are Central Standard
Time.)

THE LION
(LEO)

REGULUS

119

constellations. On a piece of level ground, the youngsters can arrange pebbles, selected carefully for size, into the various constellations' shapes. Make them big and dramatic.

For individual or tabletop maps, use sheets of paper and place seeds of various sizes to indicate the stars in the sky.

Official star maps often appear in newspapers. Large ones, showing the heavens at different seasons of the year, may be bought very inexpensively from bookstores, or from the American Museum of Natural History, 81st Street and Central Park West, New York, New York 10024. They're excellent incentives for locating and identifying the stars.

Astronomers and their laboratories are located in observatories. Some will allow visitors to inspect their telescopes and domes. Others conduct tours and give lectures. Try to visit one of the best known, which are listed below; it's a thrilling experience.

OBSERVATORIES

Lowell Observatory, Flagstaff, Ariz.
Lick Observatory, Mount Hamilton, Calif.
Mount Palomar Observatory, Mount Palomar, Calif.
Mount Wilson Observatory, Mount Wilson, Calif.
High Altitude Observatory, Climax, Colorado
U.S. Naval Observatory, Washington, D.C.
Dearborn Observatory, Evanston, Ill.
Goethe Link Observatory, Brooklyn, Ind.
Harvard College Observatory, Cambridge, Mass.
Observatory of the University of Michigan, Ann Arbor, Mich.
McMath-Hulbert Observatory, Lake Angelus, Mich.
Princeton Observatory, Princeton, N.J.
Sacramento Peak Observatory, Sunspot, New Mexico
Rutherford Observatory, Columbia University, New York, N.Y.
Perkins Observatory, Delaware, Ohio
Sproul Observatory, Swarthmore, Pa.
McDonald Observatory, Mount Locke, Texas
Leander McCormick Observatory, Charlottesville, Va.
Yerkes Observatory, Williams Bay, Wisconsin

RESOURCES

No prices have been indicated for any of the material listed in the following section, because prices change frequently. The reader is advised to check by letter with any of the publishers and other sources mentioned, requesting the latest publication lists and the current prices.

Books

All Children Have Gifts. Washington, D.C.: Association for Childhood Education International, 1965.
Guidelines for seeking resources within every child—scientific, technical, social, academic; classroom examples.

CARLSON, BERNICE WELLS. *Listen! And Help Tell the Story.* New York: Abingdon Press, 1965.
Stories in which children can participate.

Children Can Make It—Experiences in the World of Materials. Washington, D.C.: Association for Childhood Education International, 1965.
Things children can make based on sound philosophy—furniture, working models, toys, musical instruments; illustrated.

CLARKE, J. F. GATES. *Butterflies.* ("A Golden Nature Guide.") New York: Simon and Schuster, 1963.
One in a series of inexpensive books on different topics. See ZIM, HERBERT S., and IRA N. GABRIELSON.

FARB, PETER. *The Story of Butterflies and Other Insects.* Irvington-on-Hudson, N.Y.: Harvey House, 1959.
Well-written for young people.

FORTINER, VIRGINIA J. *Archaeology as a Hobby.* Maplewood, N.J.: C. S. Hammond and Co., 1962.
Interesting book to arouse interest in the past.

GOTTSCHO, SAMUEL. *A Pocket Guide to Wildflowers.* New York: Washington Square Press, 1960.
Nice to have around for quick identification.

GRIMM, WILLIAM CARY. *Pocket Field Guide to Trees.* Harrisburg, Pa.: Stackpole Books, 1958.
Basic information for tree identification. Sketches showing leaves, flowers, bark, twigs, etc.

HAMMETT, CATHERINE T. *Your Own Book of Campcraft.* ("Pocket Book" 50043.) New York: Affiliated Publishers, 1964.
An excellent paperback for use by young people.

ICKIS, MARGUERITE. *Nature in Recreation* (rev. ed.). New York: A. S. Barnes and Co., 1965.
Introducing nature through camping, handcraft, games, dramatics, music, dance and aquatics.

KNOBEL, BRUNO. *101 Camping Out Ideas and Activities.* New York: Sterling Publishing Co., 1961.
Includes firemaking, trail signs, stars, codes, and other phases of camp activities.

MALLAN, LLOYD. *Satellites as a Hobby.* Maplewood, N.J.: C. S. Hammond and Co., 1962.
An interesting book to arouse the interest of young scientists.

MARTIN, CURTIS. *The Story of Shells.* Irvington-on-Hudson, N.Y.: Harvey House, 1956.
The how and why in simple language.

MUSSELMAN, VIRGINIA W. *The Day Camp Program Book—An Activity Manual for Counselors.* New York: Association Press, 1963.
A book full of programs and activities suitable for camp and outdoor setting.

NICHELSBURG, JANET. *The Nature Program at Camp—A Book for Camp Counselors.* Minneapolis: Burgess Publishing Co., 1960.
Describes various types of nature programs at different kinds of camps.

OSBORN, BEN. *Introduction to the Outdoors.* Washington, D.C.: Audubon Naturalist Society of the Central Atlantic States, 1965.
Excellent, stimulating material, not too difficult for easy use.

PETERSON, ROGER TORY. *A Field Guide to the Birds.* New York: Houghton Mifflin Co., 1934.
A must for all birders.

PETERSON, ROGER TORY. *Pocket Field Guide to Animal Tracks.* Harrisburg, Pa.: Stackpole Books, 1958.
Identification of footprints of most of our animals with an accurate sketch of each. Pertinent data on characteristics, identification, habitat, range, food, breeding and usefulness to man.

PRICE, BETTY. *Adventuring in Nature.* Washington, D.C.: National Recreation and Park Association, 1958.
A paperback book of ideas for nature activities in all seasons.

SCHMIDT, KARL P., and D. DWIGHT DAVIS. *Field Book of Snakes.* New York: G. P. Putnam's Sons, 1941.
Excellent for reference and for use in identification.

Science for the Eights-to-Twelves. Washington, D.C.: Association for Childhood Education International, 1965.
Photos illustrate observations and experiences. Includes listing of content areas by experts. Planning for learning; selected materials.

TEALE, EDWIN WAY. *Junior Book of Insects.* New York: E. P. Dutton & Co., 1953.
Interesting, and written in simple language.

VAN DER SMISSEN, BETTY, and OSWALD H. GOERING. *A Leader's Guide to Nature-Oriented Activities.* Ames: Iowa State University Press, 1965.
> Types of activities: crafts, games, outdoor living skills, projects and hobbies, outing sports, campfire programs, family and day camping, Indian lore, winter activities.

VINAL, WILLIAM ("Cap'n Bill") GOULD. *Nature Recreation—Group Guidance for the Out-of-Doors* (2d ed.). New York: Dover Publications, 1963.
> A new edition of an old classic.

WELLS, ROBERT. *Bird Watching as a Hobby.* Maplewood, N.J.: C. S. Hammond and Company, 1962.
> How to attract, feed and identify birds.

WELLS, ROBERT. *Weather Forecasting as a Hobby.* Maplewood, N.J.: C. S. Hammond and Co., 1962.
> Simple, interesting material, useful for all young weathermen.

ZIM, HERBERT S., and ALEXANDER C. MARTIN. *Flowers.* ("A Golden Nature Guide.") New York: Simon and Schuster, 1950.
> One of an excellent, inexpensive series.

ZIM, HERBERT S., and ALEXANDER C. MARTIN. *Trees.* ("A Golden Nature Guide.") New York: Simon and Schuster, 1956.
> Another in a fine series of inexpensive nature books.

ZIM, HERBERT S. and CLARENCE COTTAM. *Insects.* ("A Golden Nature Guide.") New York: Simon and Schuster, 1951.
> Another inexpensive and excellent nature book.

ZIM, HERBERT S., and IRA N. GABRIELSON. *Birds.* ("A Golden Nature Guide.") New York: Simon and Schuster, 1949.
> Still another in the excellent "Golden Nature Guide" series.

Magazines

National Geographic Magazine, published by National Geographic Society, 17th and M Sts., N.W., Washington, D.C. 20036 (monthly).

Natural History, published by American Museum of Natural History, Central Park W. at 79th St., New York, N.Y. 10024 (monthly).

Nature and Science, published by American Museum of Natural History, Central Park W. at 79th St., New York, N.Y. 10024 (fortnightly).

Organizations

American Camping Association, Bradford Woods, Martinsville, Indiana 46151.
> Camp and day camp standards, camp directories and general information in field of camping.

American Museum of Natural History, Department of Insects and Spiders, Central Park W. at 79th St., New York, N.Y. 10024.
Free leaflets on nets, collecting and rearing insects, and the like.

Association for Childhood Education International, 3615 Wisconsin Ave., N.W., Washington, D.C. 20016.
Excellent, inexpensive publications. See Books.

Audubon Society, 1130 Fifth Ave., New York, N.Y. 10028.
Excellent resource on all aspects of nature, not birds only.

Boy Scouts of America, New Brunswick, N.J. 08903.
The famous Handbook makes a useful resource tool for all nature leaders.

Camp Fire Girls, 65 Worth Street, New York, N.Y. 10013.
Excellent material on conservation and other aspects of nature.

Cornell University Press, 124 Roberts Place, Ithaca, N.Y. 14850.
Excellent long-playing records of bird calls, insect calls, calls of frogs and toads, and sounds of nature. Listings available.

Girl Scouts of the U.S.A., 830 Third Ave., New York, N.Y. 10022.
Excellent source for nature material suitable for girls.

Golden Press, Inc., Rockefeller Center, 630 Fifth Ave., New York, N.Y. 10020.
Distributes the "Adventure Book Series": (rocks, birds, leaves, weather, sea shells, insects, stars, nature craft, underwater life, forest wonders), all inexpensive, well-illustrated and interesting.

Keep America Beautiful, 99 Park Ave., New York, N.Y. 10016.
Resource for anti-litter ideas, and for beautification campaigns.

National Safety Council, 425 North Michigan Ave., Chicago, Ill. 60611.
Inexpensive leaflets in safety topics such as bicycle safety tests, fire and accident prevention, pedestrian safety, playground safety, highway safety signs, etc.

National Wildlife Federation, 1412 16th St., N.W., Washington, D.C. 20036.
Good resources for bird, animal and other stamps, and for general nature material. Publishes *National Wildlife* magazine, a bimonthly, for members. Membership $5 a year.

Alphabetical Index of Games and Activities

ABC hunt, 93
Accident cases, 102
Acorn people, 64
Act-a-smell, 40
Adventure trails, 97
Alive show-and-tell, 48
Alphabet, 46
Anatomy, 58
Anemometer, 108
Animal anatomy, 51
Animal babies, 50
Animal feelers, 33
Animal groups, 50
Animal homes, 50
Animals—male and female, 50
Animal sounds, 51
Barometer, 110
Bell ringer, 28
Bird, the, 52
Bird caller, 72
Bird's-eye view, 19
Birds fly, 29
Birds' opera house, 31
Bird tree, 19
Blind game, 33
Blindman's cane, 27
Blind taster, 36
Bow-wow, 26
Bring-them-back-alive trip, 98
Bug's-eye view, 19
Butterfly hunt, 64
Buzzy B's, 65
Camouflage, 23
Categories, 45
Child's View, 19
Chivas, 74
Clouds, 112
Color family, 21
Color tours, 20
Color trickery, 21
Color walks, 101
Color wheel, 21
Construction engineers, 45
Daisy take, 82
Deer stalking, 26
Design, 21
Did you know???, 114
Dinosaur egg hunt, 91
Disappearing dime, 23
Ducky lucky, 28
Earthworm, the, 52
Eye-openers, 17
Feather, a, 52
Feelings, 33
Find my flower, 61
Find the leader, 16
Finger identification, 34
Finger memory, 34
Fish-eye view, 19
Flight watch, 19
Flower puzzle, 61
Food for thought, 57
Food fun, 43
Fooling feel, 32
Four in a row, 76
Fox and geese, 76
French blindman's buff, 25
Friendship sticks, 71
From where I sit, 47
Go get it, 48
Gold rush, 64
Grab bag, 34

Grass prints, 65
Guess-whats, 17
Hares and hounds, 99
Harness race, 27
Hearing vocabulary, 31
Horizontal club, 31
Huff and puff designs, 22
Indian hike, 31
Individual nature hunt, 93
I see a color, 20
I spy, 16
Jack's alive, 75
Javelin throw, 71
Jingling match, 26
Jungle paths, 78
Kick stick, 67
Kick the stick, 75
Leaf snatch, 61
Let's look and see, 51
Let-them-alone hunt, 94
Listening corner, post, tree or lean-to, 31
Locomotive walk, 102
Look-or-find-out quiz, 56
Lost in the woods, 82
Memory test, 18
Nature alphabet, 62
Nature calendar, 62
Nature charades, 47
Nature collage, 63
Nature gossip, 48
Nature's discards, 100
Nature's toys, 63
Nature's travelers, 43
Nature's zoo, 100
Neighborhood treasure hunt, 90
Newspaper weather maps, 110
Nimble nine, 78
Nine-men's morris, 69
Nosey walk, 40
Observation projects, 115
Oddities, 100
Onion hunt, 40
Op art, 22
Outdoor smelling, 40
Parasites, 100
Penny-wise, 18
Pickup stick, a, 73
Pick up sticks, 62
Pinpointed, 77
Pitfalls, 101
Planets, the, 115
Progressive hike, 101
Quests, 99
Rabbit, the, 52
Rabbit hunt, 67
Rainbow hunt, 98
Rain gauge, 111
Right whites, 18
Rubber band whistle, 72
St. Swithin's Day weather chart, 113
Scavenger hunts, 92
Secret numbers, 88
Shake the keys, 26
Shape hunt, 94
Sharp eyes, 16
Sky diver, 65
Snap board, 69
Snatch the keys, 26
Sniffer quiz, 39
Solar system, the, 114
Sound dropping, 29
Sound waves, 29

Space ship and satellite, 62
Speed limits, 52
Square meal, a, 44
Stake your claim, 63
Stalking, 28
Star maps, 117-120
Star projects, 117
Star trick, 81
Statues, 16
Stick around, 74
Still pond, no more moving, 27
Storing nuts, 75
String-alongs, 22
Sundials, 114
Sunny- and rainy-day bags, 113
Tag day, 101
Tastings, 37
Thermometer, the, 112
Toy gardens, 72
Trail reading, 98
Trail throwaways, 98
Treasure hunts, 87
Treasure walks, 98
Tree bingo, 47
Tree claims, 100
Tree tag day, 45

Tree trailing, 97
Tree treasure hunt, 91
Tricky touch, 35
Triple sight, 23
Trips and walks, 97
True or false, 55
Twig Teaser I, 79
Twig Teaser II, 79
Verbalizing taste, 37
Verbalizing touch, 34
Walnut shell mice, 65
Watermelon hunt, 91
Weather flags, 109
Weather vanes, 108
Weight-guessing, 33
What do you think? 54
What is smell? 39
What tree am I? 56
Where is taste? 37
Whistling contest, 30
Who's your friend? 18
Wind, 107
X marks the spot, 81
You're It, 71

Index of Games by Type

Blindfold Games
  Blind game, 33
  Blindman's cane, 27
  Blind taster, 36
  Bow-wow, 26
  Deer stalking, 26
  Ducky lucky, 28
  Find the leader, 16
  Finger identification, 34
  Finger memory, 34
  French blindman's buff, 25
  Grab bag, 34
  Harness race, 27
  Jingling match, 26
  Shake the keys, 26
  Snatch the keys, 26
  Stalking, 28
  Statues, 16
  Still pond, no more moving, 27
  Tricky touch, 35
Designs, Games Based on
  Camouflage, 23
  Huff and puff designs, 22
  String-alongs, 22
Hearing, Games Based on
  Bell ringer, 28
  Birds' opera house, 31
  Blindman's cane, 27
  Bow-wow, 26
  Deer stalking, 26
  Ducky lucky, 28
  French blindman's buff, 25
  Harness race, 27
  Hearing vocabulary, 31
  Horizontal club, 31
  Indian hike, 31
  Jingling match, 26
  Listening corner, post, tree or lean-to, 31
  Shake the keys, 26
  Snatch the keys, 26
  Sound dropping, 29
  Sound waves, 29
  Stalking, 28
  Still pond, no more moving, 27
  Whistling contest, 30

Identification, Games Based on
  Animal anatomy, 51
  Animal babies, 50
  Animal groups, 50
  Animal homes, 50
  Animals—male and female, 50
  Animal sounds, 51
  Bird, the, 52
  Bring-them-back-alive trip, 98
  Construction engineers, 45
  Earthworm, the, 52
  Find my flower, 61
  Flower puzzle, 61
  Go get it, 48
  Individual nature hunt, 93
  Leaf snatch, 61
  Let's look and see, 51
  Let-them-alone hunt, 94
  Nature alphabet, 62
  Nature calendar, 62
  Nature gossip, 48
  Nature's discards, 100
  Parasites, 100
  Quests, 99
  Rabbit, the, 52
  Shape Hunt, 94
  Trail throwaways, 98
  Tree tag day, 45
Improvised materials, games using
  Acorn people, 64
  Anemometer, 108
  Barometer, 110
  Bell ringer, 28
  Bird caller, 72
  Bird tree, 19
  Butterfly hunt, 64
  Buzzy B's, 65
  Chivas, 74
  Daisy take, 82
  Dinosaur egg hunt, 91
  Finger identification, 34
  Friendship sticks, 71
  Gold rush, 64
  Grass prints, 65
  Huff and puff designs, 22
  Javelin throw, 71

Jungle paths, 78
Kick stick, 67
Kick the stick, 75
Nature calendar, 62
Nature collage, 63
Nature's toys, 63
Nimble nine, 78
Nine-men's morris, 69
Op art, 22
Pickup stick, a, 73
Pick up sticks, 62
Rabbit hunt, 67
Rain gauge, 111
Rubber band whistle, 72
St. Swithin's Day weather chart, 113
Sky diver, 65
Snap board, 69
Sound waves, 29
Space ship and satellite, 62
Star maps, 117-120
Star projects, 117
Stick around, 74
Storing nuts, 75
String-alongs, 22
Sundials, 114
Sunny- and rainy-day bags, 113
Toy Gardens, 72
Walnut shell mice, 65
Weather flags, 109
Weather vanes, 108
Observation, Games Based on
Accident cases, 102
Adventure trails, 97
Alive show-and-tell, 48
Animal feelers, 33
Barometer, the, 110
Bird, the, 52
Bird's-eye view, 19
Birds fly, 29
Bird tree, 19
Bug's-eye view, 19
Camouflage, 23
Child's view, 19
Clouds, 112
Color family, 21
Color tours, 20
Color trickery, 21
Color walks, 101
Color wheel, 21
Construction engineers, 45
Disappearing dime, 23
Earthworm, the, 52
Eye-openers, 17
Feather, a, 52
Find the leader, 16
Fish-eye view, 19
Flight watch, 19
Food fun, 43
From where I sit, 47
Go get it, 48
Gold rush, 64
Guess-whats, 17
Hares and hounds, 99
Individual nature hunt, 93
I see a color, 20
I spy, 16
Let's look and see, 51
Let-them-alone hunt, 94
Locomotive walk, 102
Look-or-find-out quiz, 56
Memory test, 18
Nature's discards, 100
Nature's travelers, 43
Nature's zoo, 100
Neighborhood treasure hunt, 90

Newspaper weather maps, 110
Observation projects, 115
Oddities, 100
Op art, 22
Parasites, 100
Penny-wise, 18
Pitfalls, 101
Planets, the, 115
Quests, 99
Rabbit, the, 52
Rainbow hunt, 98
Rain gauge, 111
Right whites, 18
St. Swithin's Day weather chart, 113
Shape hunt, 94
Speed limits, 52
Stake your claim, 63
Star projects, 117
Statues, 16
Sundials, 114
Tag day, 101
Thermometer, the, 112
Treasure walks, 98
Tree claims, 100
Tree tag day, 45
Tree trailing, 97
Tree treasure hunt, 91
Triple sight, 23
True or false, 55
Watermelon hunt, 91
Weather flags, 109
What do you think? 54
Who's your friend? 18
Pantomime Games
Act-a-smell, 40
Nature charades, 47
Tastings, 37
You're It, 71
Pencil-and-Paper Games
Alphabet, 46
Categories, 45
Fox and geese, 76
Jungle paths, 78
Lost in the woods, 82
Pinpointed, 77
Rabbit hunt, 67
Square meal, a, 44
Star trick, 81
Tree bingo, 47
True or false, 55
What tree am I? 56
X marks the spot, 81
You're It, 71
Puzzles
Color trickery, 21
Daisy take, 82
Disappearing dime, 23
Fooling feel, 32
Four in a row, 76
Lost in the woods, 82
Nimble nine, 78
Pinpointed, 77
Square meal, a, 44
Star trick, 81
Tricky touch, 35
Triple sight, 23
Twig Teaser I, 79
Twig Teaser II, 79
X marks the spot, 81
Quizzes
Anatomy, 58
Did you know???, 114
Eye-openers, 17
Food for thought, 57

Guess-whats, 17
Look-or-find-out quiz, 56
Penny-wise, 18
Sniffer quiz, 39
True or false, 55
What do you think?, 54
What tree am I?, 56
Sky, Games Associated with the,
Did you know???, 114
Planets, the, 115
Star maps, 117-120
Star projects, 117
Sundials, 114
Smell, Games Based on,
Act-a-smell, 40
Food fun, 43
Nosey walk, 40
Onion hunt, 40
Outdoor smelling, 40
Sniffer quiz, 39
What is smell?, 39
Sound, Games Based on,
Animal sounds, 51
Bird caller, 72
Rubber band whistle, 72
Taste, Games Based on
Blind taster, 36
Food fun, 43
Tastings, 37
Verbalizing taste, 37
Where is taste? 37
Touch, Games Based on
Blind game, 33
Feelings, 33
Finger identification, 34
Finger memory, 34
Food fun, 43
Fooling feel, 32
Grab bag, 34
Let's look and see, 51
Tricky touch, 35
Verbalizing touch, 34
Weight-guessing, 33
Trips, Walks, and Hunts
ABC hunt, 93
Accident cases, 102
Adventure trails, 97
Bird's-eye view, 19
Birds' opera house, 31
Bring-them-back-alive trip, 98
Butterfly hunt, 64
Buzzy B's, 65
Clues, 87
Color tours, 20
Color walks, 101
Dinosaur egg hunt, 91
Flower puzzle, 61
Gold rush, 64
Hares and hounds, 99
Indian hike, 31
Individual nature hunt, 93
Let-them-alone hunt, 94
Listening corner, post, tree or lean-to, 31
Nature alphabet, 62
Nature collage, 63
Nature's discards, 100
Nature's toys, 63
Nature's travelers, 43
Nature's zoo, 100

Neighborhood treasure hunt, 90
Nosey walk, 40
Oddities, 100
Onion hunt, 40
Outdoor smelling, 40
Parasites, 100
Pitfalls, 101
Quests, 99
Rainbow hunt, 98
Shape hunt, 94
Tag day, 101
Trail throwaways, 98
Treasure walks, 98
Tree claims, 100
Tree tag day, 45
Tree treasure hunt, 91
Watermelon hunt, 91
Verbalization, Games Based On
ABC hunt, 93
Adventure trails, **97**
Alive show-and-tell, 48
Alphabet, 46
Animal anatomy, 51
Animal babies, 50
Animal groups, 50
Animal homes, 50
Animals—male and female, 50
Animal sounds, 51
Bird tree, 19
Categories, 45
Clouds, 112
Color family, **21**
Color tours, 20
Color walks, 101
Color wheel, 21
Construction engineers, 45
Flight watch, 19
Food fun, 43
Friendship sticks, 71
From where I sit, 47
Hearing vocabulary, 31
Nature's travelers, 43
Nosey walk, 40
Outdoor smelling, 40
Trail throwaways, 98
Tree bingo, 47
Verbalizing taste, 37
Verbalizing touch, 34
What do you think?, 54
Weather, Games Based on
Clouds, 112
Newspaper weather maps, 110
Rain gauge, 111
St. Swithin's Day weather chart, 113
Sunny- and rainy-day bags, 113
Thermometer, the, 112
Wind, Games Based on
Anemometer, the, 108
Weather flags, 109
Weather vanes, 108
Nature recordings, 30
Nature: value and need, 9-11, 14, 15, 25, 32, 36, 39, 42, 49, 60, 67, 74, 86, 96, 106, 107, 114
Observatories, 120
Planetariums, 117
Planets, 115-116
Resources, 120-124
Summer star maps, 118-119